Country Kitchens
& Recipes

Landhausküchen
& Rezepte

Les Cuisines romantiques
& Recettes

Country Kitchens
& Recipes

Landhausküchen
& Rezepte

Les Cuisines romantiques
& Recettes

Barbara & René Stoeltie

EDITED BY · HERAUSGEGEBEN VON · SOUS LA DIRECTION DE

Angelika Taschen

TASCHEN

KÖLN LONDON MADRID NEW YORK PARIS TOKYO

CONVERSION TABLE

WEIGHT		LIQUID		BUTTER		FLOUR	
30 g	1 oz	100 ml	3 ½ fl oz · scant ½ cup	25 g	1 oz · 2 tablespoons	50 g	2 oz · ½ cup
100 g	3 ½ oz	125 ml	4 fl oz · ½ cup	50 g	2 oz · 4 tablespoons	125 g	4 ½ oz · 1 ¼ cups
150 g	5 oz	150 ml	5 fl oz · ⅔ cup	75 g	3 oz · 6 tablespoons	150 g	6 oz · 1 ½ cups
175 g	6 oz	250 ml	9 fl oz · 1 cup	100 g	3 ½ oz · ½ cup	200 g	7 oz · 2 cups
300 g	10 oz	350 ml	12 fl oz · 1 ½ cups	150 g	6 oz · ¾ cup	250 g	9 oz · 2 ½ cups
350 g	12 oz	500 ml	18 fl oz · 2 ¼ cups	300 g	10 oz · 1 ½ cups	275 g	10 oz · 2 ¾ cups
400 g	14 oz			450 g	18 oz · 2 ¼ cups	450 g	17 ½ oz · 4 ½ cups
500 g	1 lb					500 g	18 oz · 5 cups
750 g	1 ½ lb						

TEMPERATURE			SUGAR	
150° C	300° F · Gas mark 2		50 g	2 oz · ¼ cup
180° C	350° F · Gas mark 4		100 g	3 ½ oz · ½ cup
200° C	400° F · Gas mark 6		150 g	5 ½ oz · ¾ cup
			250 g	9 oz · 1 ¼ cups

LENGTH	
0.5 cm	0.2 in
8 cm	3.2 in

All metric to British/U.S.
measurements are approximate.

© 2002 TASCHEN GmbH
Hohenzollernring 53, D–50672 Köln
www.taschen.com

Design by Catinka Keul, Cologne
Layout by Angelika Taschen, Cologne
Texts edited by Susanne Klinkhamels, Cologne
English translation by Anthony Roberts, Lupiac
German translation by Stefan Barmann, Cologne

Printed in Italy
ISBN 3–8228–1379–6 (edition with English cover)
ISBN 3–8228–1380–x (edition with French cover)
ISBN 3–8228–1374–5 (edition with German cover)

PAGE 2: *the Commanderie de Lavaufranche, in France, and its mediaeval kitchen.*

SEITE 2: *die Komturei von Lavaufranche in Frankreich mit ihrer mittelalterlichen Küche.*

PAGE 2: *la Commanderie de Lavaufranche, en France, et sa cuisine médiévale.*

CONTENTS
INHALT
SOMMAIRE

"You never recover from your youth," wrote Colette, and she was right: I know very well that my own life was shaped forever by the childhood years I spent in the house where I was born. Growing up around Cordula, my Flemish great grandmother, I vividly remember her big country kitchen, a high-ceilinged, dark room with broad grey flagstones in which the central feature was a pot-bellied cast-iron stove. This was Cordula's kingdom, filled with her cooking pots and the scent of her delicious stews.

I was fascinated by Cordula, always dressed in black, her belly bulging under a long check apron. I can still see her in my mind's eye, invariably bent over a copper saucepan or over her kitchen table whose pale wood surface, washed and scrubbed ad infinitum, seemed to gleam like satin. As a little girl I used to stand on tiptoe watching Cordula's daily show, as she chopped her vegetables, trussed her chickens and soaked thin slices of bread in milk. These would later be moved to a bowl full of whipped egg yolks, before being transformed by the venerable oven into a bread pudding topped with a thick layer of caramelised brown sugar.

Everything Cordula knew about cooking she had learned from her mother, and Cordula's own mother had learned everything from her mother. They came from a long line of robust, broad-shouldered peasant women with apple cheeks and big hands reddened by years of hard work; hands that had learned at an early age to paint their kitchen walls with whitewash cut with indigo to keep the flies away. They sprinkled sand on the floor around the stove to protect the floor from splashes of hot oil, butter and lard, and they had the knack of concocting simple, healthy, succulent dishes, such as Cordula's "jardinières" of peas and slightly sweetened carrots, her farm chicken with chicory, her cinnamon-flavoured "poires etuvées", her celebrated twisted and puffed

LANDHAUSKÜCHEN DER WELT

»Von seiner Jugend erholt man sich nie«, schrieb Colette, und sie hatte Recht: Ich weiß nur zu gut, dass mein eigenes Leben für immer durch meine Kindheit geprägt ist, die ich in dem Haus verbrachte, in dem ich geboren wurde. Ich wuchs auf in der Welt Cordulas, meiner flämischen Urgroßmutter, und erinnere mich lebhaft an ihre große Landhausküche, einen grau gefliesten, dunklen Raum mit hoher Decke, in dem ein bauchiger gusseiserner Herd die zentrale Stelle einnahm. Dies war Cordulas Königreich, gefüllt mit ihrem Kochgeschirr und dem Duft ihrer köstlichen Schmorgerichte.

Cordula, stets in Schwarz gekleidet, den Bauch gewölbt unter der langen karierten Schürze, faszinierte mich. Ich sehe sie noch vor meinem geistigen Auge, stets über eine kupferne Stielkasserolle oder über ihren Küchentisch gebeugt, dessen helle, wieder und wieder gewaschene und gescheuerte Holzoberfläche wie Satin schimmerte. Als kleines Mädchen verfolgte ich auf Zehenspitzen stehend Cordulas tägliche Vorführung – wie sie Gemüse schnitt, die Hühner dressierte und dünne Brotscheiben in Milch einlegte. Die wanderten später in eine Schüssel mit geschlagenem Eidotter, ehe daraus in dem ehrwürdigen Herd ein Brotpudding entstand, der von einer dicken Schicht karamellisiertem braunen Zucker überzogen war.

Alles, was Cordula vom Kochen wusste, hatte sie von ihrer Mutter erfahren, wie auch diese alles von der ihren gelernt hatte. Sie entstammte einer langen Ahnenreihe stämmiger, breitschultriger Bauersfrauen mit Apfelbäckchen und großen, in Jahren harter Arbeit geröteten Händen, die frühzeitig gelernt hatten, die Küchenwände mit indigohaltiger Tünche zu streichen, um die Fliegen fern zu halten. Rund um den Herd streuten diese Frauen Sand auf den Boden, um ihn vor den heißen Fettspritzern zu schützen. Sie waren geübt darin, einfache, gesunde und leckere Gerichte zu bereiten: zum Beispiel Cordulas »jardinières« mit Erbsen und leicht gesüßten Möhren, ihr Bauernhofhühnchen mit Chicorée, ihre mit Zimt abgeschmeckten »poires étuvées«, ihre berühmten »croquettes«

LES CUISINES ROMANTIQUES DU MONDE ENTIER

«On ne guérit jamais de sa jeunesse», écrivait Colette et j'avoue que mon enfance a été marquée par le souvenir de ma maison natale. Ayant grandi dans le giron de Cordula, mon arrière-grand-mère flamande, je me souviens vivement avoir passé mes premières années dans une grande cuisine rustique où trônait un poêle en fonte ventru. C'est ici que Cordula veillait en souveraine sur sa batterie de cuisine et sur ses délicieux petits plats mijotés.

Comment décrire cette pièce haute et sombre et dont le sol était recouvert de grandes dalles grises? Comment expliquer l'attrait que j'éprouvais pour Cordula, toujours vêtue de noir, son ventre rebondi sous un long tablier à carreaux. Je la revois, penchée invariablement sur une casserole en cuivre ou sur sa table de cuisine dont la surface en bois clair, lavée et récurée mille fois avec une brosse en chiendent, était lustrée comme du satin. Toute petite, je me tenais sur la pointe des pieds pour ne rien manquer du «spectacle» et pour la regarder découper ses légumes, brider le poulet et faire tremper dans du lait les fines tranches de pain de mie qui, tout à l'heure, baigneraient dans un bol rempli de jaunes d'œufs avant de se transformer dans son vieux poêlon en un «pain perdu» onctueux couvert d'une couche épaisse de cassonade caramélisée.

Cordula avait tout appris de sa mère, et celle-ci tout de la sienne. Ces robustes paysannes bien charpentées, aux pommettes saillantes et dont les grosses mains rougeâtres trahissaient la rude existence avaient appris à badigeonner les murs de leurs cuisines à la chaux en y ajoutant une pincée de teinture indigo pour chasser les mouches. Elles avaient appris à saupoudrer de sable fin les dalles autour de leur poêle pour protéger le sol des éclaboussures d'huile, de beurre et de saindoux. Et elles avaient appris à concocter des plats simples, sains et succulents.

Restent gravés dans ma mémoire les «jardinières» de petits pois et de jeunes carottes légèrement sucrés de Cordula, ainsi que son poulet fermier aux endives, ses poires étuvées parfumées à la cannelle, ses célèbres «croquettes» tordues et bour-

"croquettes" with their light dusting of powdered sugar, and her inimitable Friday evening soup, which she simmered for hours on the stove, enveloping the kitchen – and the rest of the house as well – with a delicate aroma of parsley, tender leeks and cloves.

Memories of a kitchen like that mark you for life. Ours, which had no frills at all, was a simple country affair whose single window was hung with rough-stitched linen curtains. The furniture consisted of a heavy pine table, with a drawer in which "mémé" (as we called Cordula) kept her murderous-looking kitchen knife, which she used to hack off slices of bread as thick as the soles of my boots. There were four stout cane-bottomed chairs, and two severe-looking dressers on whose broad shelves sat bright plaster figures of Jesus, Mary and Joseph, mingled with assorted plums in armagnac, brandied cherries, gherkins pickled in tarragon-flavoured vinegar and jams made of quince, raspberry and redcurrant. Cordula also maintained an extensive array of home remedies, which she swore by: she had scores of small bottles and phials hidden away in the kitchen. There was melted snow for the complexion, a mixture of egg yolks and "eau de vie" for burns, sachets of bicarbonate of soda for stomach aches, Haarlem oil for colic, and "eau des Carmes" – applied with an eye dropper to lumps of sugar – for soothing the nerves.

At the end of the corridor leading to the kitchen was the pantry, a kind of cupboard set into the wall whose depth and darkness for some reason filled me with dread. Here Cordula kept the food with which she nourished her family. In a big bowl of white earthenware were fresh eggs, often with soft chicken down still sticking to them; an enameled tin jug contained our boiled milk, protected with a damp cloth from intruding flies, spiders and the effects of thunderstorms – for Cordula firmly believed electricity in the air could turn milk sour. Here and there

aus gezwirbeltem Blätterteig, bestäubt mit Puderzucker, und ihre unnachahmliche Freitagabendsuppe, die stundenlang auf dem Herd simmerte und dabei die Küche – und das Haus gleich mit – in einen delikaten Duft von Petersilie, zartem Lauch und Nelken hüllte.

Erinnerungen an eine Küche wie diese prägen einen fürs Leben. Die unsere war eine schlichte Bauernküche, an deren einzigem Fenster grob bestickte Leinenvorhänge hingen. Das Mobiliar bestand aus einem schweren Kieferntisch mit einer Schublade, in der »mémé« – so nannten wir Cordula – das mörderisch aussehende Küchenmesser aufbewahrte, mit dem sie dicke Brotscheiben absäbelte. Es gab vier robuste Stühle mit geflochtener Sitzfläche und zwei streng anmutende Anrichten, auf deren Ablagen leuchtende Gipsfiguren von Jesus, Maria und Josef standen, in einträchtiger Gesellschaft mit Pflaumen in Armagnac, Kirschen in Branntwein, Gurken in Estragonessig sowie Marmeladen aus Quitten, Stachelbeeren und roten Johannisbeeren. Cordula unterhielt auch ein ausgedehntes Sortiment an Hausmitteln, auf die sie schwor: Dutzende von Fläschchen und Phiolen hatte sie in ihrer Küche verborgen. Da gab es geschmolzenen Schnee für den Teint, eine Mixtur aus Eidotter und »eau de vie« für Verbrennungen, Tütchen mit Natron gegen Bauchschmerzen.

Am Ende des Ganges zur Küche befand sich die Vorratskammer, eine Art in die Wand eingelassener Schrank, dessen Tiefe und Dunkelheit mich aus irgendeinem Grund mit Furcht erfüllte. Hier bewahrte Cordula die Speisen auf, mit denen sie ihre Familie ernährte. In einer großen Steingutschale lagen frische Eier, an denen oft noch Hühnerfedern klebten; ein emaillierter Zinnkrug enthielt gekochte Milch, mit einem feuchten Tuch vor Fliegen und Spinnen, aber auch vor den Folgen von Gewittern geschützt – denn Cordula war fest davon überzeugt, dass Milch durch Elektrizität in der Luft sauer werden könne. Da und dort standen Körbe mit roten Zwiebeln, Birnen und runzligen Äpfeln, hinzu kam gelegentlich

souflées qu'elle saupoudrait d'une neige de sucre glace et son inimitable «potage du vendredi soir» qui mijotait pendant des heures sur le poêle, embaumant la cuisine – et le reste de la maison – de l'arôme délicat du persil, des jeunes poireaux et des clous de girofle.

Grandir dans une cuisine ancienne vous marque pour la vie. La nôtre, sans luxe aucun, n'était qu'une simple cuisine de campagne dont la seule fenêtre s'ornait de rideaux «bonne femme» en lin grossièrement cousus. Elle était meublée d'une lourde table en pin équipée d'un tiroir où Mémé gardait un véritable couteau d'assassin avec lequel elle découpait des tranches de pain grosses comme les semelles de mes bottines, de quatre chaises paillées très solides et peu gracieuses et de deux armoires buffets aux lignes sévères, dont les larges étagères abritaient des effigies en plâtre polychrome de l'enfant Jésus, de la vierge Marie et de saint Joseph et un amoncellement de bocaux contenant des prunes à l'Armagnac, des cerises à l'eau-de-vie, des cornichons au vinaigre et à l'estragon et des confitures de quetsches, de fraises et de groseilles à maquereau. Côté «pharmacie», Cordula ne jurait que par ses propres recettes et, au fond de ses tiroirs, à côté du tire-bouchon, de l'écumoire et des cuillers en bois, elle gardait un pêle-mêle extraordinaire de flacons et de fioles. De la neige fondue pour le teint brouillé, un mélange de jaunes d'œuf et d'eau-de-vie pour les brûlures, des sachets de bicarbonate de soude pour les maux d'estomac, de l'huile de Haarlem pour faire passer les coliques et de l'eau des Carmes – administrée au compte-gouttes sur un morceau de sucre – pour apaiser les crises de nerf.

Au bout du corridor qui menait à la cuisine, le garde-manger, une sorte d'armoire encastrée sombre et profonde (et qui m'inspirait une peur inexplicable) abritait de quoi nourrir sa famille. Dans un grand bol en faïence blanche, Mémé gardait ses œufs tout frais auxquels collait encore souvent le duvet délicat du postérieur de la poule et, dans une cruche en métal émaillé, elle gardait le lait bouilli qu'un linge mouillé proté

were baskets filled with red onions, pears and wrinkled apples, with the odd mouldy-smelling bunch of radishes. But what really caught my attention as a little girl was the china butter-dish, whose cover had a pink-footed cow lolling on top of it, so enchanting that I never missed an opportunity to stroke her little head with its curled-back horns.

Nostalgia alters things, expanding and embellishing what we remember. That modest kitchen seems huge to me when I look back on it. Were the walls really covered with pious images and 1900 portraits representing the members of our all-too-numerous family? And did "mémé" really have a rattan armchair wherein she rested after the effort of preparing a stew of rabbit simmered in beer, or a "boeuf bourguignon à la moutarde" flavoured with bay leaves? Our memories can play tricks. I'm still in the habit of claiming that Cordula's pig's feet with prunes and brown sugar were the best on the planet – much to people's amusement. The young laugh even harder when I declare that milk used to taste twice as good, and reminisce about the beauty of our old Louvain stove, with its gentle murmur and its interlacing noodle patterns. Nevertheless I still silently tell myself that I'm right, that our grandmothers' kitchens were really special affairs, and even now there's no better place to cook than between four lime-washed walls, using copper pans that reflect the image of a stout, fiery-cheeked peasant woman. So away with your electrical gadgets, forget the laboratory kitchen in which the cooking of an egg is reduced to a sterile, inhuman act, tie on your apron, bring out your wooden ladle, check dishcloths and iron pot. Set to work with a will, while yet you can.

ein modrig riechender Bund Rettich. Was aber als kleines Mädchen meine besondere Aufmerksamkeit erweckte, war eine Butterdose aus Porzellan, deren Deckel mit einer rosafüßigen Kuh verziert war, die ich so bezaubernd fand, dass ich keine Gelegenheit ausließ, ihr Köpfchen mit den nach hinten gebogenen Hörnern zu streicheln.

In der Nostalgie verändern sich die Dinge, erweitern und verschönern sich unsere Erinnerungen. Die bescheidene Küche scheint mir im Rückblick weitläufig. Waren die Wände wirklich mit Andachtsbildern und Porträts von den Mitgliedern unserer vielköpfigen Familie bedeckt? Und hatte »mémé« wirklich einen Sessel aus Rohrgeflecht, in dem sie sich ausruhte, nachdem sie ein in Bier geköcheltes Kaninchenragout oder einen mit Lorbeerblättern aromatisierten »bœuf bourguignon à la moutarde« zubereitet hatte? Unser Gedächtnis spielt uns manchen Streich. Ich behaupte nach wie vor, dass Cordulas Schweinshaxen mit Pflaumen und braunem Zucker die besten der Welt waren – sehr zur Erheiterung der anderen. Noch lauter lachen die jungen Leute, wenn ich erkläre, die Milch habe damals doppelt so gut geschmeckt, und in Erinnerungen an die Schönheit unseres alten wallonischen Ofens mit seinem sanften Summen und seinem geflochtenen Nudelmuster schwelge. Trotzdem sage ich mir immer im Stillen, dass ich Recht habe und die Küchen unserer Großmütter wirklich etwas Besonderes waren: Noch heute gibt es keinen besseren Ort zum Kochen, als zwischen vier gekälkten Wänden mit Kupferpfannen zu hantieren, in denen sich das Bild einer kräftigen, rotwangigen Bauersfrau spiegelt. Lassen wir sie also beiseite, die elektrischen Geräte, vergessen wir die Laborküche, in der das Kochen eines Eis zu einem sterilen, inhumanen Akt herabgewürdigt wird. Ziehen wir die Schürze an und holen wir das Holzbrett, karierte Geschirrtücher und den eisernen Topf hervor. Machen wir uns an die Arbeit, solange noch Zeit dazu ist.

geait des mouches, des araignées et aussi des effets de l'orage et du tonnerre censés le faire «tourner». Ci et là traînaient des paniers remplis d'oignons rouges, de poires et de pommes ratatinées ou d'une botte de radis sentant le moisi. Mais ce qui a surtout retenu l'attention de la petite fille que j'étais, ce fut le beurrier en porcelaine dont le dessus était orné d'une vache couchée au pie rose: je la trouvais si mignonne que je ne ratais aucune occasion de caresser sa petite tête ornée d'une paire de cornes gentiment recourbées.

On dit que la nostalgie transforme, agrandit ou embellit les souvenirs, et il est vrai que cette cuisine modeste me semble immense aujourd'hui. Et puis, les murs étaient-ils vraiment recouverts d'images pieuses et de portraits «1900» représentant les membres de notre famille trop nombreuse? Mémé avait-elle vraiment un fauteuil en rotin dans lequel elle se reposait après avoir préparé avec amour un civet de lapin à la bière ou un bœuf bourguignon à la moutarde piqué de feuilles de laurier.

La mémoire vous joue des tours. D'ailleurs aujourd'hui je me rends souvent ridicule en prétendant que les pieds de porc aux pruneaux et à la cassonade de Cordula étaient les meilleurs au monde. Je vois sourire «les jeunes» quand je vante le goût onctueux du lait d'antan, le charme du vieux poêle dit «de Louvain» avec son ventre rouge ronronnant et ses ornements «style nouille». Et puis je me dis tout bas que c'est moi qui ai raison, que les cuisines de nos grands-mères avaient de quoi faire rêver et qu'il fait bon cuisiner entre quatre murs badigeonnés à la chaux dans des casseroles en cuivre qui renvoient le reflet d'une grosse paysanne aux joues en feu. Rangez vos gadgets mécaniques, ignorez le laboratoire dans lequel cuire un œuf ressemble à un acte stérile et inhumain, enfilez un tablier et armez-vous d'une louche en bois, d'un torchon à carreaux et d'une cocotte en fonte. Au travail, avant qu'il ne soit trop tard …

The French designer
Franck Evennou and
his wife Marianne
painted the walls of
their kitchen yellow, to
give it a sunny atmos-
phere; the curtains are
a cheery bright red.

Um ihr eine sonnige
Atmosphäre zu geben,
haben der französische
Designer Franck Even-
nou und seine Frau
Marianne die Wände
ihrer Küche gelb ge-
strichen; die Vorhänge
sind in strahlendem,
heiteren Rot gehalten.

Le créateur français
Franck Evennou et sa
femme Marianne ont
badigeonné les murs de
leur cuisine en jaune
pour lui donner un
air ensoleillé et confec-
tionné de gais rideaux
rouge vif.

An old set of kitchen coppers lined up on shelves is both decorative and highly practical in this big Swedish kitchen.

So dekorativ wie praktisch ist das auf Borden aufgereihte alte Kupfergeschirr in dieser geräumigen schwedischen Küche.

Une ancienne batterie de cuisine en cuivre, posée sur des étagères, est à la fois décorative et très pratique dans cette vaste cuisine suédoise.

Ochre walls are perfect for Jean and Dorothée d'Orgeval's pretty Provencal kitchen. To achieve something similar, you'll need the same natural pigments mixed with animal glue.

Ockerfarbene Wände passen perfekt in die provenzalische Küche von Jean und Dorothée d'Orgeval. Um einen solchen Anstrich zu erzielen, mischt man natürliche Pigmente mit Glutinleim.

Ces murs ocre vont à merveille avec la jolie cuisine provençale de Jean et Dorothée d'Orgeval. Pour réaliser un décor semblable loin du beau pays de Mistral, on utilise des pigments naturels et de la colle de peau.

An 18th century Dutch
kitchen, which owes
much of its magic to
traditional colours such
as the fresh butter hue
of the panelling. This
can still be found today
in specialist paint shops.

Viel von ihrem Zauber
verdankt diese nieder-
ländische Küche aus
dem 18. Jahrhundert
den traditionellen Far-
ben, so dem »frischen
Butter«-Ton der Täfe-
lung, der noch heute
in Spezialgeschäften
erhältlich ist.

Cette cuisine hollandai-
se 18ᵉ doit beaucoup de
sa magie aux couleurs
traditionnelles, tel le
ton «beurre frais» des
boiseries. Il est disponi-
ble de nos jours dans les
magasins spécialisés.

This 18th-19th century Dutch kitchen offers a straightforward palette of colours, marrying geranium red with cobalt blue (supposed to repel flies) and a fireplace decorated with Delft tiles.

Diese niederländische Küche aus dem 18. und 19. Jahrhundert bietet eine klar zusammengesetzte Farbpalette aus Geranienrot und Kobaltblau (das, so sagt man, Fliegen fern hält) sowie einen mit Delfter Kacheln verkleideten Kamin.

Cette cuisine hollandaise des 18ᵉ et 19ᵉ siècles offre une palette franche qui marie le rouge géranium au bleu cobalt (réputé chasser les mouches) et une cheminée dont le foyer est recouvert de carreaux de Delft.

The occupants have carefully preserved the period details of this magnificent kitchen in the heart of Tuscany: rustic furniture, copper utensils and limewashed walls.

Sorgfältig haben die Bewohner darauf geachtet, die historischen Besonderheiten dieser großartigen Küche im Herzen der Toskana zu erhalten: rustikale Möbel, Kupfergerät und gekälkte Wände.

Les habitants ont préservé jalousement les détails d'époque de cette magnifique cuisine située au cœur de la Toscane: meubles rustiques, ustensiles en cuivre et murs crépis à la chaux.

At the Chateau de la Ferté Saint-Aubin, Jacques and Catherine Guyot have recreated a typical 17th century kitchen with period utensils and a game rack hung with hams, sausages and stuffed animals.

Auf Schloss La Ferté Saint-Aubin haben Jacques und Catherine Guyot mit historischen Einrichtungsgegenständen und am Balken aufgehangenen Schinken, Würsten und Tierpräparaten eine Küche im typischen Stil des 17. Jahrhunderts nachgestaltet.

Au château de La Ferté Saint-Aubin, Jacques et Catherine Guyot ont recréé une cuisine typiquement 17ᵉ en y intégrant des ustensiles d'époque et en chargeant la tringle à gibier de jambonneaux, de saucissons et d'animaux naturalisés.

At the Chateau de Drée
in France's Brionnais,
the kitchen has changed
little since the old days.
Anne Prouvost and her
husband delight their
visitors with their col-
lection of tin jugs and
a massive 19th century
cast iron cooking range.

Im Schloss Drée im
Brionnais sieht die
Küche immer noch aus
wie in alten Zeiten.
Anne Prouvost und ihr
Ehemann erfreuen die
Besucher mit ihrer
Sammlung von Zinn-
krügen und dem impo-
santen gusseisernen
Küchenherd aus dem
19. Jahrhundert.

Au château de Drée,
dans le Brionnais, la
cuisine a gardé son
aspect d'antan. Anne
Prouvost et son époux
font la joie des visiteurs
en y exposant des pichets
en fer blanc et une
impressionnante cuisi-
nière en fonte 19ᵉ.

In the Commanderie de Lavaufranche, the Wattel family's vast collection of old country furniture and earthenware and tin utensils has a setting that is worthy of it.

Die umfangreiche Sammlung von alten Bauernmöbeln, Terrakotta- und Zinnobjekten der Familie Wattel hat in der Komturei von Lavaufranche einen würdigen Rahmen gefunden.

Dans la Commanderie de Lavaufranche, la vaste collection de meubles rustiques anciens et d'ustensiles en étain et en faïence de la famille Wattel a trouvé un décor digne d'elle.

In this Stockholm attic, the designer Martine Colliander has created a kitchen using modern elements while respecting the dominant shade of white and the red brick of the floor.

In einem Stockholmer Dachgeschoss hat die Designerin Martine Colliander eine traditionelle Küche mit modernen Elementen eingerichtet, wobei sie dem dominierenden Weiß und dem Ziegelsteinboden Rechnung trug.

Dans un grenier à Stockholm, la créatrice Martine Colliander a su créer une cuisine à l'ancienne avec des éléments assez récents tout en respectant la dictature du blanc et la brique rouge du sol.

PREPARING MEALS & RECIPES

The preparation of a meal is usually accompanied by sustained activity: pleasurable anticipation at the prospect of going to market, then the march along the lines of stalls, scrutinizing, touching and sniffing the products soon to be made into a delicious meal. Back in the kitchen, the baskets are emptied on the table, in a picturesque but evanescent still life: a fine green cabbage, for example, a fish with scales glinting gold, a crusty baguette and a stack of fresh herbs.

To prepare a meal is to honour tradition. In the drawer of an old cupboard slumbers the cook's bible: a school exercise book filled with culinary treasures painstakingly assembled by an ancestor who left the prints of buttery fingers – and the odd splash of sauce, whose original you remember well and have tried in vain to imitate. If the kitchen walls could speak, they would tell of aromatic stocks murmuring in the broad copper casserole, of the squeak of garlic cloves tossed in hot foamy butter, of the daily tussle between the cook, her utensils and her ingredients, of familiar gestures, cries of triumph, wails of despair.

To give away a secret recipe is tantamount to an act of love. Since the dawn of time, cooks' mysteries have been passed down orally and from notebook to notebook, to arrive at last before the eyes of yet another woman looking to delight her family with a grand new dish.

MAHLZEITEN ZUBEREITEN & REZEPTE

LA PREPARATION DU REPAS & LES RECETTES

Die Zubereitung einer Mahlzeit ist meist mit gesteigerter Aktivität verbunden: angefangen bei der Vorfreude, auf den Markt zu gehen, bis zum Umherstreifen zwischen den Ständen, wo die Erzeugnisse, die sich bald darauf in ein köstliches Gericht verwandeln sollen, in Augenschein genommen, betastet und berochen werden. Zurück in der Küche, werden die Körbe auf dem Tisch ausgeleert, sodass ein pittoreskes, aber kurzlebiges Still-Leben entsteht: ein zarter Grünkohl zum Beispiel, ein Fisch mit goldglitzernden Schuppen, ein knuspriges Baguette und ein Strauß frischer Kräuter.

Ein Mahl zu bereiten, heißt die Tradition zu ehren. In der Schublade eines alten Schranks schlummert die Bibel der Köchin: ein Schulheft voller kulinarischer Schätze, sorgfältigst zusammengestellt von einer Vorfahrin, die darin die Abdrücke buttriger Finger hinterlassen hat – und den einen oder anderen Spritzer einer Sauce, die man in guter Erinnerung hat und vergeblich nachzuahmen sucht. Könnten die Küchenwände sprechen, sie würden von würzigen Bouillons erzählen, vom Zischen der Knoblauchzehen in der heiß aufschäumenden Butter und vom täglichen Gerangel zwischen der Köchin, ihren Gerätschaften und Ingredienzien, von vertrauten Handreichungen, Rufen des Entzückens und Tränen der Verzweiflung.

Ein geheimes Rezept weiterzugeben, kommt einem Akt der Liebe gleich. Seit Urzeiten werden Küchengeheimnisse mündlich überliefert und von Notizbuch zu Notizbuch abgeschrieben, bis sie vielleicht bei einer Köchin landen, die ihre Familie mit einem echten Schmaus überraschen will.

Préparer un repas est souvent accompagné d'une activité frénétique, et qui ne connaît pas le frisson exquis que l'on éprouve à se rendre au marché, se promener le long des étals aguichants et scruter, tâter et humer les produits qui, tout à l'heure, se transformeront en un repas succulent. De retour à la cuisine, le contenu des paniers s'entasse sur la table, composant une nature morte pittoresque où domine bien souvent le chou vert décoratif, le poisson aux reflets d'argent, les bottes de fines herbes et la baguette croustillante.

Cuisiner c'est aussi honorer une tradition. Dans le tiroir d'une vieille armoire dort la bible de la cuisinière: un cahier d'écolière rempli de trésors culinaires jalousement rassemblés par une aïeule qui y a laissé les empreintes grasses de ses doigts et quelques éclaboussures d'une sauce qu'on a essayé en vain d'imiter, au moins, cent fois. Si les murs des cuisines savaient parler, ils nous raconteraient les gestes familiers, l'odeur du bouillon qui murmure dans la grande marmite en cuivre, le bruit des gousses d'ail qui crient dans le beurre écumant et la lutte quotidienne qui s'instaure entre la cuisinière, ses outils et ses ingrédients, entrecoupée de cris de triomphe et de larmes de désespoir.

Livrer le secret d'une recette est un acte d'amour. Depuis l'aube des temps, les mystères de la cuisine passent de bouche à oreille et de cahier en cahier pour aboutir chez la cuisinière en herbe désireuse de surprendre les siens par un plat aux allures d'offrande.

STARTERS

VORSPEISEN

ENTREES

Nut bread
Nussbrot
Pain aux noix

500 g flour
1 teaspoon salt
3 teaspoons yeast
1 egg
80 g sugar
110 g crushed nuts
Milk (enough to obtain
a smooth mixture, at
room temperature)

Butter a cake mould and bring the oven to medium heat (120 C). Mix together the flour, salt, sugar and yeast. Add the nuts. Mix well.

Make a hole in the middle of the mixture and incorporate the egg and enough milk to make a smooth, soft mass (make sure you have plenty of milk, because the nuts will absorb a lot of liquid). Knead the dough well for a few minutes, then put it aside for 20 minutes.

Empty the mixture into the mould and bake in the oven for 3–4 hours, or until the bread is golden, with a firm, light consistency and a well-aerated interior. (no illustration)

500 g Mehl
1 TL Salz
3 TL Backpulver
1 Ei
80 g Zucker
110 g gehackte Nüsse
Milch (Raumtempera-
tur; genug, um einen
glatten Teig herzustel-
len)

Buttern Sie eine Kuchenform aus und heizen Sie den Backofen auf mittlerer Stufe (120° C) vor. Vermengen Sie Mehl, Salz, Zucker und Backpulver. Geben Sie die Nüsse hinzu. Nochmals gut durchmischen.

In der Mitte der Mischung legen Sie eine Mulde an und fügen das Ei sowie genügend Milch hinzu, sodass eine homogene, glatte Masse entsteht (da die Nüsse viel Flüssigkeit aufsaugen, sollten Sie genug Milch bereithalten). Kneten Sie die Masse ein paar Minuten lang gut durch und lassen Sie sie anschließend etwa 20 Minuten ruhen.

Den Teig in die Form geben und 3–4 Stunden im Ofen backen. Das Brot soll goldbraun aussehen, eine feste, aber luftige Konsistenz haben und innen locker sein. (ohne Abbildung)

500 g de farine
1 c. à café de sel
3 c. à café de levure chi-
mique
1 œuf
80 g de sucre
110 g de noix concassées.
Lait (assez pour obtenir
un mélange lisse –
température ambiante)

Beurrez un moule à cake et chauffez le four à température moyenne (120° C). Mélangez la farine, le sel, le sucre et la levure. Ajoutez les noix. Mélangez bien.

Faites un puits au centre du mélange et incorporez l'œuf et suffisamment de lait pour obtenir une masse homogène, lisse et onctueuse (prévoyez assez de lait car les noix absorbent beaucoup de liquide.) Pétrissez bien la pâte pendant quelques minutes et laissez la reposer ensuite pendant 20 minutes.

Versez le mélange dans le moule et faites cuire au four pendant 3 à 4 heures. Le pain doit être doré, avoir une consistance ferme et légère avec une mie bien aérée. (sans illustration)

HERRING FILLETS WITH DILL
HERINGSFILETS MIT DILL
FILETS DE HARENG A L'ANETH

*2 herring fillets
per person
450 g butter
4 eggs
450 g flour
750 g potatoes
4 tablespoons of
fresh cream
Nutmeg
Handful of finely-
chopped dill
Salt and pepper*

Separate yolks from whites, then beat the yolks well and add a pinch of salt. Coat the fillets in egg yolk, then toss them briefly in a paper bag full of flour. Place the floured fillets on a dish (not touching) and put aside. Next make ordinary mashed potatoes, preferably using a hand purée machine so the mixture is not too creamy; add cream, pepper, salt and nutmeg to taste and leave in the oven to keep warm.
Heat the butter in a pan and when it is very hot fry the fillets quickly. When done, sprinkle them generously with dill and serve on big plates, with the mashed potatoes doused in melted butter. Best accompanied by a cold Scandinavian lager beer. (no illustration)

*2 Heringsfilets
pro Person
450 g Butter
4 Eier
450 g Mehl
750 g Kartoffeln
4 EL Crème fraîche
Muskatnuss
Eine Handvoll fein
gehackter Dill
Salz und Pfeffer*

Die Dotter vom Eiweiß trennen und mit einer Prise Salz kräftig durchschlagen. Tauchen Sie die Herings-filets in die Eidottermasse und bemehlen Sie sie (am einfachsten geben Sie sie mit dem Mehl in eine große Papiertüte und schütteln kurz durch). Legen Sie die Filets anschließend nebeneinander auf einen Teller (sie sollten sich nicht berühren). Bereiten Sie ein klassisches Kartoffelpüree zu, am besten mit dem Kar-toffelstampfer, damit die Masse nicht zu kremig wird. Crème fraîche unterziehen, mit Pfeffer, Salz und Muskatnuss abschmecken und bei mittlerer Hitze im Ofen warm stellen.
Lassen Sie die Butter in einer Pfanne sehr heiß werden und sautieren Sie darin die Heringe. Aus der Pfanne nehmen und großzügig mit Dill bestreuen. Auf großen Tellern anrichten und das reichlich mit zerlassener Butter beträufelte Püree hinzugeben. Am besten passt dazu ein kaltes skandinavisches Lagerbier. (ohne Abbildung)

*2 filets de hareng
par personne
450 g de beurre
4 œufs
450 g de farine
750 g de pommes de
terre
4 c. à soupe de crème
fraîche
Noix de muscade
Une poignée d'aneth
finement haché
Sel et poivre*

Séparez les jaunes des blancs et battez les jaunes vigoureusement en ajoutant une pincée de sel. Trempez les filets de hareng dans le jaune d'œuf avant de les fariner (facile si on les place avec la farine dans un grand sac en papier que l'on secoue dans tous les sens). Posez les filets sur un plat, sans les superposer, et mettez de côté. Faites une purée de pommes de terre classique (en employant un presse-purée pour éviter d'obtenir une masse trop crémeuse), ajoutez la crème fraîche, le poivre, le sel et la noix de muscade et tenez la purée au chaud dans un four moyen.
Faites chauffer le beurre dans la poêle et quand il est très chaud, déposez-y les filets de hareng que vous faites cuire à feu vif. Hors de la poêle, saupoudrez-les généreusement avec l'aneth. Faites ensuite fondre un grand morceau de beurre dans une casserole et servez les filets dans de grandes assiettes avec la purée généreusement arrosée de beurre fondu. Les filets de hareng à l'aneth apprécient la compagnie d'une bière – scandinave – blonde et froide. (sans illustration)

Terrine of smoked salmon with dill
Lachsterrine mit Dill
Terrine de saumon fumé à l'aneth

Serves 6 to 8 people:
750 g smoked salmon
3 leaves gelatin, or
30 g powdered gelatin
Juice of one lemon
100 ml warm water
100 g cream cheese
Bunch of dill
250 ml unskimmed
fresh milk
350 ml fresh cream
(whipped)
1 egg white (beaten till
stiff)
Black pepper (12 turns
of the peppermill) and a
pinch of Cayenne pepper

Soak the gelatin leaves in a little warm water. Line a terrine dish with slices of salmon, then put the remaining salmon in the mixer with the lemon juice and pepper, to obtain a smooth blend; add the milk and the cream cheese and mix again. Gently heat the water and gelatin until the gelatin is dissolved. Allow to cool for 15 minutes, pour over the salmon mixture and blend. Next, empty the salmon into a bowl and carefully fold in the whipped cream, the finely-chopped dill and the beaten egg white. Pour the resultant mousse into the terrine and leave for 24 hours in the refrigerator. Before serving, place the terrine dish in boiling water for a moment; this makes it easier to turn the mousse onto a plate. Slice and serve.

Für 6 bis 8 Personen:
750 g geräucherter Lachs
in Scheiben
3 Blätter Gelatine oder
30 g Gelatinepulver
Saft von einer Zitrone
100 ml lauwarmes Wasser
100 g Sahnequark
1 Bund Dill
250 ml frische Vollmilch
350 ml Crème fraîche
(geschlagen)
1 Eiweiß (zu Schnee
geschlagen)
Pfeffer (12 Mühlen-
drehungen) oder eine
Prise Cayenne-Pfeffer

Weichen Sie die Gelatineblätter im lauwarmen Wasser ein. Belegen Sie den Boden einer Terrinenform mit der Hälfte der Lachsscheiben. Den Lachs für die Füllung mit Zitronensaft und Pfeffer im Mixer pürieren bis die Masse glatt ist. Milch und Quark zugeben und weitermixen. Wasser und Gelatine in einem kleinen Topf vorsichtig erhitzen, bis die Gelatine aufgelöst ist. 15 Minuten abkühlen lassen, über die Lachsmasse geben und mischen. Jetzt geben Sie den Lachs in eine Schüssel und ziehen behutsam die Crème fraîche, den fein gehackten Dill und das geschlagene Eiweiß unter. Die Mousse in die Form füllen, mit den übrigen Lachsscheiben belegen und das Ganze 24 Stunden im Kühlschrank ruhen lassen. Vor dem Servieren die Form kurz in sehr heißes Wasser tauchen, sodass sich die Terrine besser stürzen lässt. In Scheiben schneiden und servieren.

Pour 6 à 8 personnes:
750 g de saumon fumé en
tranches
3 feuilles de gélatine ou
30 g de gélatine en poudre
Le jus d'un citron
100 ml d'eau tiède
100 g de fromage blanc
crémeux
Une botte d'aneth
250 ml de lait entier
350 ml de crème fraîche
(fouettée)
1 blanc d'œuf (battu en
neige)
Poivre (12 tours de
moulin) ou une pincée
de Cayenne

Trempez les feuilles de gélatine dans l'eau tiède. Foncez et garnissez un moule à terrine avec les tranches de saumon. Passez le reste du saumon au mixeur avec le jus de citron et le poivre, jusqu'à obtention d'une masse lisse. Sans cesser de tourner, ajoutez le lait puis le fromage blanc afin d'obtenir une masse crémeuse. Mettez le mélange d'eau et de gélatine dans une petite casserole et chauffez doucement pour dissoudre la gélatine. Laissez refroidir pendant 15 minutes, versez le liquide sur la crème de saumon et mélangez le tout. Placez le saumon dans une jatte et incorporez-y avec précaution la crème fraîche fouettée, l'aneth finement haché et le blanc d'œuf battu en neige. Déposez la mousse de saumon dans la terrine, couvrez avec les tranches de saumon et laissez reposer 24 heures au réfrigérateur. Démoulez en plongeant la terrine pendant quelques instants dans de l'eau très chaude, coupez en tranches et servez.

Shrimp croquettes
Krabbenkroketten
Croquettes aux crevettes

For 4 to 6 people:
150 g shrimps
500 g potatoes
150 g breadcrumbs
Bunch of parsley
Pepper and salt
2 eggs
50 g flour
Fat for deep-frying

Boil the potatoes with a little parsley in a big saucepan of salted water. When they are cooked, drain, remove the parsley, mash well and allow to cool. Add the eggs, beat the mixture into a smooth, light paste and put aside to cool. Chop four sprigs of parsley and add to the mixture along with the shrimps. Add pepper and salt to taste. (Take care not to add the shrimps to the purée while it is still hot, as this will dry them out.) Divide the mixture into small balls, then place on a floured surface and shape into cylinder-shaped croquettes. Roll croquettes in breadcrumbs and allow to stand for several hours in a cool place or in the refrigerator. To cook, heat a mixture of beef dripping and horse fat in a frying pan – this is the original recipe, but if you can't obtain these ingredients use ordinary frying oil. The fat should be very hot (180 C): test heat by putting in one croquette to see how it does, before adding the rest. When the croquettes are well browned, remove with a skimming utensil and drain on a paper towel before serving. Garnish with freshly-chopped parsley and lemon quarters.

Für 4 bis 6 Personen:
150 g geschälte Krabben
500 g Kartoffeln
150 g Paniermehl
1 Bund Petersilie
Salz und Pfeffer
2 Eier
50 g Mehl
Fett zum Frittieren

Die Kartoffeln in einer großen Kasserolle mit zwei bis drei Zweigen Petersilie in Salzwasser gar kochen. Danach abgießen, abkühlen lassen und durch die Pürierpresse drücken. Schlagen Sie die Masse mit den Eiern zu einem glatten, lockeren Püree, das Sie abkühlen lassen. Vier Zweige fein gehackte Petersilie und die Krabben hinzufügen. Salzen und pfeffern. (Das Püree darf nicht mehr heiß sein, sonst trocknen die Krabben aus.) Aus der Mischung rollen Sie kleine Bällchen, setzen diese auf eine mit Mehl bestäubte Fläche und bringen sie in zylindrische Form. Anschließend in Paniermehl wälzen und einige Stunden an einem kühlen Ort (Kühlschrank) ruhen lassen. Erhitzen Sie eine Mischung aus gleichen Teilen Rinderschmalz und Pferdefett – so empfiehlt es das Originalrezept, möglich ist aber auch gewöhnliches Frittieröl. Das Öl muss sehr heiß sein (ca. 180° C). Ob die Hitze stark genug ist, testen Sie mit einer einzelnen Krokette, die Sie auf einem langen Löffel eintauchen. Wenn die Kroketten goldbraun sind, mit der Schaumkelle herausnehmen, vor dem Servieren auf Küchenpapier entfetten, mit geviertelten Zitronen und frittierter Petersilie garnieren.

Pour 4 à 6 personnes:
150 g de crevettes décor-
tiquées
500 g de pommes de terre
150 g de chapelure
1 botte de persil
Poivre et sel
2 œufs
50 g de farine
Matière grasse pour
friture

Faites cuire les pommes de terre accompagnées de deux à trois branches de persil dans une grande casserole remplie d'eau salée. Lorsqu'elles sont cuites, égouttez-les, ôtez les brins de persil, laissez refroidir et passez-les au presse-purée. Ajoutez les œufs, battez pour obtenir une purée lisse et légère et laissez refroidir à nouveau. Ajoutez ensuite quatre brins de persil finement hachés et les crevettes. Poivrez et salez. Formez des boulettes de purée, roulez-les dans la farine en essayant de leur donner une forme cylindrique, puis dans la chapelure. Laissez reposer les croquettes pendant quelques heures dans un endroit frais ou au réfrigérateur. Faites chauffer la graisse dans la friteuse. La graisse doit être très chaude (180° C environ). Faites un essai en y plongeant une petite croquette. Retirez avec une écumoire quand les croquettes sont bien dorées. Servez avec un demi citron par personne et – si possible – des brins de persil frits.

MAIN
COURSES

HAUPT-
GERICHTE

PLATS
PRINCIPAUX

BLANQUETTE DE VEAU

For 6 people:
1 kg breast of veal
cut in large pieces
150 g salted farm
butter
4 large onions
(or a dozen shallots)
Flour
1 glass dry white wine
4 carrots
125 ml fresh cream
1 lemon
300 g mushrooms
(preferably oyster
mushrooms)
Bouquet garni
(1 leek, thyme, parsley,
bay leaf, tied together
with string)
Salt and pepper
3 egg yolks

For the meatballs:
400 g minced veal,
and if possible 400 g
white boudin (veal
sausage) preferably
flavoured with truffles

Brown the pieces of meat in a cast iron pot if you have one. Sprinkle with flour until the meat takes on a russet colour, then add white wine and enough water to cover; stock or fond de boeuf may also be used. Bring to the boil, then simmer for 2 hours.

In another saucepan, place 1 spoonful of butter, the onions, the carrots chopped into rounds, the mushrooms and the bouquet garni, and allow to simmer over a low flame for 20 minutes. Then add the meatballs and cook slowly for a further 15 minutes. Now add the veal sausages if you have them, remove from the fire and keep warm.

When the meat is sufficiently tender (it should melt in the mouth) remove from the flame and make a thick sauce with butter, flour, the cooking juices and fresh cream. Remove the pot from the flame before vigorously beating the egg yolks into this sauce, adding the juice of one lemon, pepper and salt as you do so.

Take a deep serving dish (or a soup tureen), put in the meat, surround it with the mixed onions, carrots, mushrooms, meatballs and veal sausages, and cover everything with the cream sauce. Serve with steamed potatoes and a cool white wine or lager beer.

Kalbsragout

Für 6 Personen:
1 kg Kalbsbrust in
großen Stücken
150 g gesalzene
Landbutter
4 Gemüsezwiebeln
(oder ein gutes
Dutzend Schalotten)
Mehl
1 Glas trockener
Weißwein
4 Karotten
125 ml Crème fraîche
1 Zitrone
300 g Pilze (vorzugs-
weise Austernpilze)
1 Bouquet garni
(1 Lauchstange,
Thymian, Petersilie
und Lorbeer, zusam-
mengebunden)
Salz und Pfeffer
3 Eidotter

Für die Fleischbällchen:
400 g Hackfleisch
sowie, wenn möglich,
400 g Weißwürste vom
Kalb, vorzugsweise
getrüffelt

Braten Sie die Fleischstücke in der Butter goldbraun an, am besten in einem gusseisernen Bräter. Streichen Sie Mehl durch ein Sieb über das Fleisch, bis es eine schöne rötliche Färbung annimmt und löschen Sie mit Weißwein und Wasser ab, bis das Fleisch bedeckt ist (Sie können auch Brühe oder Rinderfonds verwenden). 2 Stunden köcheln lassen.

Geben Sie ein Nüsschen Butter in eine weitere Kasserolle, fügen Sie die Zwiebeln, die in Scheiben geschnittenen Karotten, die Pilze und das Bouquet garni hinzu, bei kleiner Hitze 20 Minuten garen. Anschließend die Fleischbällchen hinzugeben und weitere 15 Minuten köcheln lassen. Falls vorhanden, kommen jetzt die Weißwürstchen dazu. Vom Feuer nehmen und warm halten.

Wenn das Fleisch gar ist (es muss auf der Zunge zergehen), nehmen Sie es vom Feuer und bereiten aus Butter, Mehl, Bratensaft und Crème fraîche eine sämige Sauce. Nehmen Sie den Topf vom Herd und rühren Sie unter kräftigem Schlagen die Eidotter unter. Mit ein wenig Zitronensaft, Pfeffer und Salz abschmecken. Das Fleisch auf eine tiefe Servierplatte (oder in eine Suppenschüssel) legen, darum die Mischung aus Zwiebeln, Karotten, Pilzen, Fleischbällchen und Würstchen drapieren und reichlich von der Sauce angießen. Mit Dampfkartoffeln und einem kühlen Weißwein oder einem hellen Bier servieren.

Blanquette de veau

Pour 6 personnes:
1 kg de poitrine de veau
coupée en gros morceaux
150 g de beurre fermier
salé
4 gros oignons
(ou une bonne douzaine
d'échalotes)
Farine
1 verre de vin blanc sec
4 carottes
125 ml de crème fraîche
1 citron
300 g de champignons
(de préférence des
pleurotes)
Bouquet garni
Sel et poivre
3 jaunes d'œuf

Pour les boulettes:
400 g de veau haché.
Eventuellement
400 g de petits boudins
blancs (de préférence
parfumés aux truffes.)

Faites dorer les morceaux de viande dans le beurre (si possible dans une cocotte en fonte), saupoudrez de farine jusqu'à ce qu'elle prenne une belle couleur rousse et mouillez avec le vin blanc et suffisamment d'eau pour que la viande soit recouverte (on peut aussi utiliser du bouillon ou un fond de bœuf). Laissez mijoter 2 heures.

Déposez dans une autre cocotte une noix de beurre, les oignons, les carottes coupées en rondelles, les champignons et le bouquet garni et laissez mijoter à feu doux une vingtaine de minutes. Ajoutez alors des boulettes de veau haché et gardez le tout encore un petit quart d'heure sur le feu. Ajoutez les petits boudins blancs, retirez du feu et gardez le tout au chaud.

Quand la viande est tendre (elle doit être fondante) retirez-la du feu et préparez un roux épais avec du beurre, de la farine, le jus de cuisson et la crème fraîche. Hors du feu, ajoutez les jaunes d'œuf en battant vigoureusement et ajoutez un peu de jus de citron, du poivre et du sel.

Prenez un plat de service profond (ou une soupière), déposez-y la viande, entourez du mélange d'oignons, de carottes, de champignons, de boulettes et de boudins et nappez généreusement avec la sauce à la crème. Servez avec des pommes de terre vapeur et un vin blanc sec frais ou une bière blanche.

OSSOBUCO ALLA GREMOLATA
OSSOBUCO ALLA GREMOLATA
OSSOBUCO A LA GREMOLATA

For 4 people:
4 veal shanks (ask your butcher to give you the thin ends, so the slices will be no broader than the palm of your hand)
250 g flour
1 lemon
300 g butter
1 bunch parsley
3 cloves peeled garlic
2 finely chopped anchovy fillets
1 glass dry white wine
Pepper and salt

Coat the shanks with flour and brown in butter in a casserole. Add the white wine, reduce it, season and allow to simmer for 2–3 hours, or until the flesh falls away from the bones. When the meat is cooked, peel the lemon and squeeze its juice into a cup. Add the lemon juice and the anchovies to the meat and sprinkle with "gremolata" – a mixture of parsley, garlic and finely chopped lemon peel. Serve the "ossobuco" with rice flavoured with saffron.

Für 4 Personen:
4 Scheiben Kalbshaxe (bitten Sie Ihren Fleischer um Stücke, die nicht breiter als eine Handfläche sind)
250 g Mehl
1 unbehandelte Zitrone
300 g Butter
1 Bund Petersilie
3 geschälte Knoblauchzehen
2 fein gehackte Anchovis-Filets
1 Glas trockener Weißwein
Pfeffer und Salz

Wenden Sie die Kalbshaxenscheiben in Mehl und braten Sie sie in der Pfanne in Butter goldbraun an. Weißwein angießen, würzen und bei milder Hitze 2–3 Stunden köcheln lassen (das Fleisch muss sich von den Knochen lösen). Wenn das Fleisch gar ist, pressen Sie die Zitrone aus und bewahren die Schale auf. Geben Sie Zitronensaft und Anchovis zum Fleisch und bestreuen Sie das Ganze mit »gremolata« – einer Mischung aus Petersilie, Knoblauch und Zitronenzesten. Servieren Sie den »ossobuco« mit Safranreis.

Pour 4 personnes:
4 tranches de jarrets de veau
250 g de farine
1 citron
300 g de beurre
1 botte de persil
3 gousses d'ail épluchées
2 filets d'anchois finement hachés
1 verre de vin blanc sec
Poivre et sel

Demandez à votre boucher de prélever les jarrets de veau dans la partie la plus mince afin que les tranches ne soient pas plus grandes que la paume de la main. Farinez les jarrets de veau et faites-les dorer au beurre dans une poêle. Ajoutez le vin blanc, faites réduire, assaisonnez et laissez mijoter à feu très doux pendant 2 à 3 heures (il faut que la chair des jarrets se détache de l'os). Quand la viande est cuite, prélevez la peau du citron avec un zesteur et recueillez le jus. Ajoutez le jus de citron et les anchois à la viande et saupoudrez le tout de «gremolata» – un mélange de persil, d'ail et de zestes de citron finement hachés. Servez «l'ossobuco» avec du riz au safran.

Irish potato cakes
Kartoffelküchlein
Galettes de pommes de terre

For 4 people:
500 g potatoes
75 g salted butter
125 g flour
Pepper and salt

Boil the potatoes in their jackets until done, then remove skins and mash by hand (do not use a mixer). Add tablespoon of melted butter and incorporate the flour until the mass detaches from the bowl and forms a smooth ball in the hands; season with pepper and salt. Roll out on a board sprinkled with flour, using a rolling pin, then use a glass to cut circles 1 cm thick and 8 cm in diameter. Sprinkle with flour, heat the rest of the butter in a pan and cook the potato cakes till they are golden brown. They may also be served hot with icing sugar or jam, to go with five o'clock tea.

Für 4 Personen:
500 g Kartoffeln
75 g gesalzene Butter
125 g Mehl
Pfeffer und Salz

Die Kartoffeln mit der Schale kochen, danach ein wenig abkühlen lassen und pellen. Anschließend durch die Püreepresse streichen (keinen Mixer verwenden). Fügen Sie einen Esslöffel zerlassene Butter hinzu und arbeiten Sie das Mehl ein, bis die Masse sich vom Gefäß löst und einen glatten Klumpen zwischen den Händen bildet. Salzen und pfeffern. Rollen Sie den Teig mit dem Nudelholz auf einem mit Mehl bestäubten Brett etwa 1 cm dick aus und stechen Sie mit einem Glas Kreise von 8 cm Durchmesser aus, die Sie in Mehl wenden. Die restliche Butter in einer Pfanne erhitzen und die Küchlein goldbraun braten. Wenn Sie möchten, können Sie sie gleich warm servieren: Mit Puderzucker oder Konfitüre passen sie gut zum Fünf-Uhr-Tee.

Pour 4 personnes:
500 g de pommes
de terre
75 g de beurre salé
125 g de farine
Poivre et sel

Faites cuire les pommes de terre avec la peau et, quand elles sont tièdes, pelez-les et passez-les au presse-purée (ne pas employer de mixeur). Ajoutez une bonne cuillerée à soupe de beurre fondu et incorporez la farine jusqu'à ce que la masse se détache de la jatte et forme une boule lisse entre les mains, poivrez et salez. Etalez sur une planche saupoudrée de farine à l'aide d'un rouleau à pâtisserie et – à l'aide d'un verre – découpez des cercles d'environ 1 cm d'épaisseur et 8 cm de diamètre. Passez-les dans la farine, faites chauffer le restant du beurre dans une poêle et faites cuire les galettes jusqu'à ce qu'elles soient bien dorées. On peut aussi les servir chaudes avec du sucre en poudre ou de la confiture pour accompagner le thé de cinq heures.

Chicken in tomato sauce
Hühnchen in Tomatensauce
Poulet a la sauce tomate

1 chicken (c. 1 kg)
4 large ripe tomatoes
3 garlic cloves
1/2 a glass extra virgin
olive oil
1 glass dry white wine
2 vanilla pods
Salt and pepper

Plunge the tomatoes in boiling water for 2–3 minutes, then place them under a cold tap: the skins will then come off without difficulty. Dice the tomatoes and put aside.

Cut the chicken into four quarters, season with salt and pepper, and brown the pieces in olive oil in a deep cast-iron pot. Add the tomatoes, the garlic, the vanilla pods and the glass of white wine. Simmer on a very low flame for 2–3 hours (the flesh should come away from the bone).

Remove the pieces of chicken from the pot and put them aside, taking care to keep them warm while you reduce the sauce, crushing the garlic cloves with a fork. Discard the vanilla pods, cover the chicken with tomato sauce, add salt and pepper if necessary and serve immediately, accompanied by potato rissoles or rice flavoured with saffron.

1 Hühnchen (ca. 1 kg)
4 große reife Tomaten
3 Knoblauchzehen
1/2 Glas Olivenöl
extra vergine
1 Glas trockener
Weißwein
2 Vanillestangen
Salz und Pfeffer

Lassen Sie die Tomaten 2–3 Minuten in kochendem Wasser ziehen und schrecken Sie sie mit kaltem Wasser ab: So lassen sie sich problemlos schälen. Zu einem Concassé verarbeiten und beiseite stellen.

Das Hühnchen in vier Stücke zerteilen, mit Salz und Pfeffer würzen und in einem tiefen gusseisernen Bräter in Olivenöl goldbraun anbraten. Fügen Sie Tomaten, Knoblauch und Vanille hinzu und gießen Sie den Weißwein an. Bei sehr milder Hitze 2–3 Stunden köcheln lassen (das Fleisch muss leicht von den Knochen zu lösen sein).

Nehmen Sie die Hühnchenteile aus dem Bräter, stellen Sie sie warm und lassen Sie die Sauce einkochen (den Knoblauch mit der Gabel zerdrücken). Die Vanillestangen entfernen, die Hühnchenstücke auf eine vorgewärmte Servierplatte geben und mit der Tomatensauce begießen. Falls nötig, nachsalzen und -pfeffern. Mit Backkartoffeln oder Safranreis servieren.

1 poulet (d'environ 1 kg)
4 grosses tomates
bien mûres
3 gousses d'ail
1/2 verre à vin d'huile
d'olive extra vierge
1 verre de vin blanc sec
2 gousses de vanille
Sel et poivre

Plongez les tomates pendant 2 à 3 minutes dans l'eau bouillante, passez-les ensuite à l'eau froide pour les peler facilement. Taillez-les ensuite en dés et mettez de côté.

Coupez le poulet en quatre, salez, poivrez et faites dorer les morceaux dans de l'huile d'olive dans une cocotte en fonte profonde. Ajoutez les tomates, l'ail, la vanille et mouillez avec le vin blanc. Laissez mijoter à feu très doux pendant 2 à 3 heures (il faut que la chair se détache facilement de des os).

Otez les morceaux de poulet de la cocotte, gardez-les au chaud et faites réduire la sauce (écrasez l'ail à la fourchette). Retirez les gousses de vanille, posez les morceaux de poulet sur un plat de service très chaud, nappez la viande de sauce tomate vanillée, rectifiez l'assaisonnement si nécessaire et servez avec des pommes de terre rissolées ou du riz au safran.

DESSERTS

DESSERTS

DESSERTS

GRIESSSCHMARREN
GRIESSSCHMARREN
GRIESSSCHMARREN

175 g semolina
1/2 litre unskimmed milk
2 tablespoons fresh cream
1 vanilla pod
2 tablespoons butter
20 g sugar
1 tablespoon dry raisins

Bring the milk to the boil in a casserole with the fresh cream, the vanilla pod, the sugar and a little butter. Remove from the flame, sprinkle in the semolina and stir vigorously. Add the raisins, cover the casserole and set aside. Preheat the oven to 150 C, butter a cake mould, pour in the cream after discarding the vanilla bean, and bake the "Griesschmarren" until golden. Remove the cake mould from the oven, break the cake surface into large pieces with two spoons, place under the grill for a few minutes until it develops a beautiful caramelised crust, then turn out on a hot serving dish and sprinkle generously with icing sugar.

175 g Grieß
1/2 Liter Vollmilch
2 EL Crème fraîche
1 Vanillestange
2 EL Butter
20 g Zucker
1 EL Rosinen

Kochen Sie die Milch mit der Crème fraîche, der Vanille, dem Zucker und einem Stückchen Butter im Topf auf. Vom Herd nehmen und unter kräftigem Rühren den Grieß einstreuen. Die Rosinen hinzugeben, den Deckel auflegen und ruhen lassen. Heizen Sie den Ofen auf 150° C vor, buttern Sie eine Kuchenform und geben Sie die Masse, aus der Sie zuvor die Vanille entfernt haben, hinein. Den Schmarren backen, bis die Oberfläche goldfarben aussieht. Dann nehmen Sie die Form aus der Röhre, zerteilen den Kuchen mit zwei Löffeln in große Stücke und stellen ihn ein paar Minuten unter den Grill, bis sich eine karamellisierte Kruste gebildet hat. Auf einer vorgewärmten Servierplatte anrichten und mit reichlich Puderzucker bestreuen.

175 g de semoule
1/2 litre de lait entier
2 c. à soupe de crème fraîche
1 gousse de vanille
2 c. à soupe de beurre
20 g de sucre
1 c. à soupe de raisins secs

Faites bouillir le lait avec la crème fraîche, la vanille, le sucre et un petit morceau de beurre. Versez hors feu la semoule en pluie et tournez vigoureusement. Ajoutez ensuite les raisins, posez le couvercle sur la casserole et laissez reposer. Préchauffez le four à 150° C, beurrez un moule à cake, versez-y la crème après avoir ôté la vanille, et faites cuire le «Griesschmarren» jusqu'à ce qu'il blondisse. Sortez le moule du four, divisez-le gâteau en gros morceaux à l'aide de deux cuillers, passez-le pendant quelques minutes sous le gril jusqu'à ce qu'il ait une belle croûte caramélisée, démoulez le tout sur un plat de service très chaud et saupoudrez généreusement de sucre en poudre.

CREMA CATALANA

500 ml unskimmed
fresh milk
250 g sugar
4 egg yolks
1 tablespoon cornflour
or potato flour
1 teaspoon powdered
cinnamon
A pinch saffron
(five or six pistils)
1 tablespoon chopped
lemon peel

Place 200 g of the sugar and the egg yolks in a bowl and beat well. Blend the potato flour in 2 tablespoons of milk, taking care to eliminate lumps. Add to the egg and sugar mixture and then incorporate the cinnamon, saffron, lemon peel and the remainder of the milk. Stir well with a wooden spoon. Pour the liquid into a saucepan and cook over a medium heat until it thickens slightly: when ready it should still drip down the ladle fairly freely.

Pour the liquid into individual oven-proof shallow cups or ramekins, allow the cream to cool, then leave the ramekins in the refrigerator for a couple of hours. When you take them out, sprinkle them with the rest of the sugar (50 g) and put them under the grill until the sugar surface caramelises to a fine dark brown. You can also buy special irons in the shape of a flat spiral, which can be used to burn the surface of the sugar very lightly, forming a thin crust which breaks like a very thin layer of glass at the touch of a spoon. A gas torch can be used for the same purpose, if you have one.

CREMA CATALANA

500 ml Vollmilch
250 g Zucker
4 Eidotter
1 EL Mais- oder
Kartoffelmehl
1 TL Zimtpulver
1 Prise (einige Fäden)
Safran
1 EL Zitronenzesten

Schlagen Sie die Eidotter mit 200 g Zucker in einer Schüssel kräftig durch. Verquirlen Sie das Mehl mit 2 EL Milch zu einer klümpchenfreien Masse und rühren Sie diese in die Zucker-Ei-Mischung. Anschließend ziehen Sie Zimt, Safran, Zitronenzesten und die übrige Milch unter. Mit einem Holzlöffel gut durchrühren, in einen Topf geben und bei mittlerer Hitze eindicken lassen – die richtige Konsistenz ist erreicht, wenn die Masse noch gut über den Löffel »läuft«.

Füllen Sie die Flüssigkeit portionsweise in ofenfeste Schälchen oder kleine Terrakotta-Schüsseln und stellen Sie diese 2 Stunden in den Kühlschrank. Anschließend mit dem restlichen Zucker (50 g) bestreuen und unter den Grill stellen, bis der Zucker dunkelbraun karamellisiert ist. Im Handel sind auch flache Spiraleisen erhältlich, mit denen der Zucker von oben leicht erhitzt wird, bis sich eine feine Kruste bildet, die bei Berührung mit dem Löffel wie eine dünne Eisschicht bricht. Ebenfalls geeignet sind Gasbrenner für den Küchengebrauch.

CREMA CATALANA

500 ml de lait entier
250 g de sucre
4 jaunes d'œuf
1 c. à soupe de maïzena
ou de fécule de pommes
de terre
1 c. à café de cannelle
en poudre
1 pincée (quelques
pistils) de safran
1 c. à soupe de zestes
de citron

Déposez 200 g de sucre et les jaunes d'œuf dans un bol et battez vigoureusement. Délayez la fécule dans 2 cuillerées à soupe de lait en évitant de faire des grumeaux. Ajoutez au mélange de sucre et d'œufs et incorporez ensuite la cannelle, le safran, les zestes de citron et le restant du lait. Remuez bien avec une cuillère en bois. Versez le liquide dans une casserole et laissez cuire à feu moyen jusqu'à ce qu'il épaississe, il doit cependant encore «couler» facilement le long de la louche.

Versez le liquide dans des coupes ou des ramequins pouvant aller au four, laissez refroidir la crème et placez les ramequins pendant deux heures au réfrigérateur. Sortez-les, versez dessus le restant du sucre (50 g) et passez les ramequins sous le gril jusqu'à ce que le sucre soit caramélisé. Le sucre doit avoir une belle couleur foncée. Il existe dans le commerce des fers en forme de spirale horizontale avec lequel le sucre est brûlé légèrement en surface, formant ainsi une croûte peu épaisse qui casse comme une couche de glace très fine au contact de la cuillère et des brûleurs spéciaux, type «lance-flammes» qui fonctionnent à l'aide d'une bonbonne de gaz.

AMERICAN APPLE PIE

For the pastry:
275 g flour
100 g lard
50 g butter
ice-cold water
1 tablespoon thick
double cream
1 teaspoon salt

For the topping:
1 kg apples
(peeled and cored,
sliced 0,5 cm thick)
25 g butter
150 g sugar
1 teaspoon lemon juice
1 tablespoon cornflour
Powdered cinnamon
Nutmeg
6 cloves
Salt

Mix the flour and the salt in a salad bowl. Gradually add the lard and butter, trying to obtain a consistency like breadcrumbs; add the ice-cold water little by little until you have a smooth, solid mass. Cover the pastry ball with a cloth and leave in the refrigerator for 1 hour.

Next, butter a shallow tin oven dish with a removable bottom, roll out the pastry on a floured board with a rolling pin and cut it in two. Lay half the pastry round the oven dish, cutting off any pieces drooping over the edges. Preheat the oven to 200 C.

In a bowl, mix the sugar, a pinch of salt, cornflour, cinnamon, cloves and 1/2 a teaspoon of freshly-ground nutmeg. Add the apples and the lemon juice and mix well with a wooden spoon. Lay slices over the pastry starting on the outside and working in a circle toward the centre. Garnish with flakes of butter, then cover with the remaining half of the pastry, taking care to fold over the excess pastry round the edges of the dish, sealing the tart lightly with your fingers and leaving decorative indentations

all round the rim. Daub the pie lightly all over with double cream, using a brush, then cut two holes in the centre of the pastry covering. Bake for 45 minutes until the crust is a deep golden colour, then serve with vanilla ice cream.

Amerikanischer Apfelkuchen

Für den Teig:
275 g Mehl
100 g Schweineschmalz
50 g Butter
Eiswasser
1 EL sehr dicke Crème
double
1 TL Salz

Für den Belag:
1 kg Äpfel
(vorzugsweise geschälte
und entkernte Renetten,
in 0,5 cm dicke Scheiben
geschnitten)
25 g Butter
150 g Zucker
1 TL Zitronensaft
1 EL Maismehl
Zimtpuder
Muskatnuss
6 Nelken
Salz

Mischen Sie Mehl und Salz in einer tiefen Schüssel. Arbeiten Sie nach und nach Schweineschmalz und Butter ein, bis die Masse eine brotkrumenartige Konsistenz hat. Dann geben Sie in kleinen Mengen Eiswasser hinzu bis der Teig homogen und glatt ist. Den Teig mit einem Küchentuch bedecken und ca. 1 Stunde im Kühlschrank ruhen lassen.

Dann buttern Sie eine Springform aus, rollen den Teig mit dem Nudelholz auf einem mit Mehl bestäubten Brett aus und schneiden zwei runde Teigplatten aus. Die Kuchenform mit der einen Teigplatte auslegen und den überstehenden Rand abschneiden. Heizen Sie den Herd auf 200° C vor.

Mischen Sie in einer Schüssel den Zucker, eine Prise Salz, das Maismehl, den Zimt, die Nelken und ein Viertel frisch geriebene Muskatnuss. Äpfel und Zitronensaft hinzugeben und das Ganze mit einem Holzlöffel gleichmäßig verrühren. Legen Sie die Apfelscheiben kreisförmig vom Rand zur Mitte auf den Teig und setzen Sie Butterflöckchen darauf. Mit der zweiten Teigplatte bedecken Sie nun den Kuchen, wobei Sie den überschüssigen Teig am Rand der Form einschlagen und den Kuchen unter leichtem Druck versiegeln, sodass die Fingerabdrücke ein dekoratives Randmuster bilden. Dann streichen Sie mit einem Pinsel die Crème double auf die obere Teigplatte und ritzen mit einem spitzen Messer zwei kleine Einschnitte in der Mitte des Kuchens. Etwa 45 Minuten backen, bis der Kuchen goldbraun ist. Mit Vanille-Eis servieren.

Tarte aux pommes a l'Americaine

Pour la pâte:
275 g de farine
100 g de saindoux
50 g de beurre
eau glacée
1 c. à soupe de crème
double très épaisse
1 c. à café de sel

Pour la garniture:
1 kg de pommes
(de préférence des
reinettes épluchées et
évidées, coupées en
tranches de 0,5 cm
d'épaisseur)
25 g de beurre
150 g de sucre
1 c. à café de jus de
citron
1 c. à soupe de maïzena
Cannelle en poudre
Noix de muscade
6 clous de girofle
Sel

Mélangez la farine et le sel dans un saladier. Ajoutez ensuite petit à petit le saindoux et le beurre en essayant d'obtenir une masse qui ressemble à des miettes de pain et ajoutez progressivement l'eau glacée afin d'obtenir une masse homogène et lisse. Couvrez la boule de pâte avec un linge et laissez reposer au réfrigérateur pendant 1 heure environ.

Beurrez un moule à tarte à fond mobile et étalez la pâte sur une planche saupoudrée de farine à l'aide d'un rouleau à pâtisserie. Formez une galette de pâte et coupez-la en deux. Foncez le moule à tarte avec la moitié de la pâte et coupez ce qui dépasse du bord. Préchauffez le four à 200° C.

Dans une jatte, mélangez le sucre, une pincée de sel, la maïzena, la cannelle, les clous de girofle et un quart de noix de muscade fraîchement râpée. Ajoutez les pommes et le jus de citron et remuez bien avec une cuillère en bois pour obtenir un mélange homogène. Déposez les tranches sur la pâte en partant de l'extérieur et en décrivant un mouvement circulaire vers le centre. Garnir de beurre en flocons. Recouvrez le tout avec la moitié restante de la pâte, en prenant soin de replier l'excès au bord du moule, de sceller la tarte légèrement avec les doigts en y laissant des empreintes pour obtenir un effet décoratif. Badigeonnez le tout de crème double à l'aide d'un pinceau et pratiquez deux incisions au centre. Laissez cuire au four pendant trois quarts d'heure jusqu'à ce que la croûte soit bien dorée et servez avec de la glace à la vanille.

CHEESECAKE

For the pastry:
200 g flour
100 g salted butter
50 g sugar
2 egg yolks
1 teaspoon almond
essence

For the topping:
750 g cream cheese
250 ml milk
150 ml thick double
cream
1 tablespoon zests
of lemon peel
Juice of one lemon
100 g sugar
25 g leaf gelatin

Pour the flour into a mixing bowl and mix in the butter. The mixture should be fairly crumbly. Add the sugar, the 2 egg yolks and the almond essence, mix well and set aside in the refrigerator for about two hours. Line a tin oven dish with a removable bottom with the mixture and bake (covered) in an oven preheated to 180 C for 20 minutes. Allow to cool.

In a bowl, mix the cheese, milk, cream, chopped lemon peel, lemon juice and sugar into a smooth blend. Immerse the leaves of gelatin in 100 ml cold water in a pan, heat gently to dissolve, then allow to cool for 15 minutes and fold carefully into the mixture. Pour this mixture into the mould and leave in a cool place for several hours. You can also cover the cake with apricot, strawberry or raspberry jam, heating the jam before you do so, allowing it to cool and pouring it through a sieve so the syrup is not too lumpy. The cake can also be sprinkled with crushed almonds just before serving.

KÄSETORTE

Für den Teig:
200 g Mehl
100 g gesalzene Butter
50 g Zucker
2 Eidotter
1 TL Mandelessenz

Für den Belag:
750 g Quark
250 ml Milch
150 g sehr dicke Crème double
1 EL Zitronenzesten
Saft einer Zitrone
100 g Zucker
25 g Blattgelatine

Geben Sie das Mehl in eine tiefe Schüssel und arbeiten Sie die Butter ein, sodass eine Mischung von krümeliger Konsistenz entsteht. Den Zucker und die beiden Eidotter sowie die Mandelessenz einkneten und etwa 2 Stunden im Kühlschrank ruhen lassen. Den Teig in einer Springform auslegen, abdecken und im auf 180° C vorgeheizten Ofen 20 Minuten backen. Abkühlen lassen.

Rühren Sie Quark, Milch, Crème double, Zitronenzesten, Zitronensaft und Zucker in einer Schüssel zu einer geschmeidigen Masse. Legen Sie die Gelatineblätter in einen Topf mit kaltem Wasser (100 ml). Behutsam erwärmen, bis sich die Blätter aufgelöst haben, 15 Minuten abkühlen und dann vorsichtig unter die Creme ziehen. Geben Sie die Mischung in die Form und stellen Sie sie ein paar Stunden lang kalt.

Man kann den Kuchen auch mit aufgekochter Aprikosen-, Erdbeer- oder Himbeermarmelade bestreichen. Etwas abkühlen lassen und durch ein Sieb streichen, um die Masse von Klümpchen zu befreien. Anschließend eventuell mit Mandelsplittern bestreuen.

Gateau au fromage

Pour la pâte:
200 g de farine
100 g de beurre salé
50 g de sucre
2 jaunes d'œuf
1 c. à café d'essence
d'amande

Pour la garniture:
750 g de fromage blanc
250 ml de lait
150 ml de crème double
très épaisse
1 c. à soupe de zestes
de citron
Le jus d'un citron
100 g de sucre
25 g de gélatine
(en feuilles)

Mettez la farine dans un saladier et incorporez le beurre. Le mélange doit rester grumeleux. Ajoutez le sucre, les 2 jaunes d'œuf et l'essence d'amande, mélangez le tout et laissez reposer au réfrigérateur pendant environ deux heures. Tapissez un moule à tarte à fond mobile avec le mélange et cuisez à couvert dans un four pré-chauffé à 180° C pendant 20 minutes. Laissez refroidir.

Dans une jatte, mélangez le fromage, le lait, la crème, les zestes de citron, le jus de citron et le sucre jusqu'à obtention d'une crème onctueuse. Disposez les feuilles de gélatine dans la casserole avec de l'eau froide (100 ml), chauffez doucement pour la dissoudre, puis laissez refroidir pendant 15 minutes et incorporez avec précaution dans la crème. Versez le mélange dans le moule et mettez-le au frais pendant quelques heures.

On peut napper le gâteau de confiture d'abricots, de fraises ou de framboises en chauffant au préalable la confiture. Laissez tiédir et passez au chinois pour éviter que le sirop soit trop grumeleux. On peut ensuite saupoudrer le gâteau d'amandes pilées.

STOVES & SINKS

"When I'm having my dinner", wrote Desaugiers in his Almanach des Gourmands, "the cook seems to me a divine being, one who governs the human race from his kitchen." But like a general who must mount his horse to govern a battlefield, the cook must have his stove and sink. Ennobled by the great chefs who named it their 'piano', the stove is the altar of Lucullus. It is upon this mute piano that we practice our scales and finger exercises, and over which we bend with burning cheeks; we load it with our copper casseroles, drawing from its cast iron box (or from the Aga cooker with its ovens and hot plates) a symphony of dishes, cakes and soufflés.

The fireplace too, with its sooty iron cauldron and smouldering embers, has always had our deep esteem, whilst the stone sink with its bulky tap appears to us immaculate. Tin sinks, too, and wooden sinks; and stoves of every kind – in a high-ceilinged Tuscan kitchen as broad as a ballroom, in Sweden, crowned by a hood as white as snow, or in Provence, blackened by burning rosemary and savory. We salute you, venerable stoves and sinks, for without you there would be neither joy nor mystery in cooking.

HERDE
& SPÜLBECKEN

FOURNEAUX
& EVIERS

»Wenn ich zu Abend speise«, schrieb Desaugiers in seinem Almanach des Gourmands, »erscheint mir der Koch als ein göttliches Wesen, das aus seiner Küche die Geschicke der Menschen lenkt«. Doch wie ein General sich auf sein Pferd schwingen muss, um das Schlachtfeld zu beherrschen, so braucht der Koch seinen Herd und seinen Spülstein. Geadelt von den großen Küchenchefs, die von ihrem »Klavier« sprachen, ist der Herd der Altar des Lukullus. Auf diesem stummen Klavier vollführen wir Tonleitern und Fingerübungen und darüber beugen wir unsere brennenden Wangen; ihn bestücken wir mit kupfernen Kasserollen und entnehmen seiner gusseisernen Röhre (oder dem AGA-Ofen mit seinen Backkammern und heißen Platten) eine Symphonie von Speisen, Kuchen und Soufflés.

Die Feuerstelle mit dem summenden gusseisernen Kessel und knisternden Holzscheit, hat uns immer schon angezogen. Und die Steinspüle mit dem großen Wasserhahn darüber erscheint uns einfach grandios. Doch begeistern können uns auch Zinn- und Holzspülen und Öfen aller Art in einer toskanischen Küche, so weit und hoch wie ein Ballsaal, in einer schwedischen, wo der Ofen von einem schneeweißen Rauchfang bekrönt ist, oder in einer provenzalischen, geschwärzt von angeschmortem Rosmarin und Bohnenkraut. Denn ohne Herde und Spülsteine gäbe es beim Kochen weder Freude noch Geheimnis.

«Un cuisinier quand je dîne, me semble un être divin qui, du fond de sa cuisine, gouverne le genre humain», écrivait Desaugiers dans son Almanach des gourmands. Mais comme un général qui ne peut se passer de son cheval pour dominer le champ de bataille et régir tout ce qui s'y passe, le cuisinier ne peut se passer de ses fourneaux et de son évier. Ennoblis par les grands chefs qui la nomment un «piano», la cuisinière devient l'autel où l'on s'adonne aux rites du divin Lucullus. De nos jours, c'est sur ce piano muet que nous faisons nos exercices et nos doigtés, penchés, les joues en feu, sur notre poêle, jouant du cuivre des casseroles, jonglant avec des crêpes et tirant de cette lourde caisse en fonte, ornée de grosses barres de cuivre (ou de l'Aga coiffé d'une paire de plaques chauffantes rutilantes) une symphonie de mets qui tout à l'heure caresseront notre palais.

L'âtre où crépite le bois et où chante la marmite en fonte a toujours eu notre sympathie. Et l'évier en pierre surmonté d'un gros robinet nous semble le comble du bonheur. Eviers en tôle, éviers en bois, fourneaux de tous les couleurs – en Toscane au cœur d'une cuisine grande et haute comme une salle de bal, en Suède, couronnés par une hotte blanche comme la neige d'un matin de Noël ou en Provence, noirs et enfumés par la fumée du romarin et de la sarriette – vous êtes indispensables à notre confort et à la beauté de nos cuisines.

STOVES
& SINKS

HERDE &
SPÜLBECKEN

FOURNEAUX
& EVIERS

PREVIOUS DOUBLE
PAGE: *In this house
an old cast iron cooker
with a brass bar and
tap gives the room its
warm and welcoming
look.*
ABOVE: *This coal-fired
cooker set in a Victorian
fireplace heats the rooms
and provides hot water
for the whole house.*

VORHERGEHENDE
DOPPELSEITE: *In
diesem Haus verleiht
ein gusseiserner Herd
mit Handumlauf und
Wasserhahn dem Raum
das typische stimmungs-
volle Ambiente.*
OBEN: *Dieser in einem
viktorianischen Kamin*

*eingelassene Kohlenherd
heizt die Räume und
versorgt das gesamte
Haus mit warmem
Wasser.*

DOUBLE PAGE
PRECEDENTE: *Dans
cette maison un ancien
«piano» en fonte orné
d'une barre et d'un
robinet de cuivre donne
à cette pièce l'ambiance
chaude et accueillante.*
CI-DESSUS: *Cette
cuisinière à charbon
encastrée dans une
cheminée victorienne
chauffe les pièces et ali-
mente la maison en
eau chaude.*

FACING PAGE:
*Franck and Marianne
Evennou have equipped
their fisherman's house
with an enameled cast
iron cooker. It still ful-
fils all their cooking
requirements.*

RECHTE SEITE:
*Franck und Marianne
Evennou haben ihr
Fischerhaus mit einem
emaillierten Gusseisen-
herd ausgestattet, der
ihren Küchenansprü-
chen noch immer voll-
auf gerecht wird.*

PAGE DE DROITE:
*Franck et Marianne
Evennou ont équipé
leur maison de pêcheur
d'une cuisinière en fonte
émaillée. Elle satisfait
pleinement leurs exigen-
ces culinaires.*

LEFT: *In their kitchen at Larchill in Ireland the owners have installed an old Aga cooker. The fireplace dates from the early 20th century.*
FACING PAGE: *Moving a 1950s enameled Aga cooker is no easy matter. The owners of this Irish cottage have opted to leave it where it is.*
FOLLOWING PAGES: *In this Dutch castle, the old stone-built oven has been covered with white Delft tiles.*

LINKS: *In ihrer Küche im irischen Larchill haben die Besitzer einen alten AGA-Herd aufgestellt. Der Kamin stammt vom Anfang des 20. Jahrhunderts.*
RECHTE SEITE: *Einen emaillierten AGA-Herd aus den 1950er Jahren von der Stelle zu bewegen, ist kein Leichtes. So beschlossen die Besitzer dieses irischen Cottages, ihn an seinem Platz zu belassen.*
FOLGENDE DOPPEL-SEITE: *In diesem holländischen Schloss wurde der alte gemauerte Ofen mit weißen Delfter Kacheln verkleidet.*

A GAUCHE: *Dans leur cuisine de Larchill en Irlande les propriétaires ont installé une cuisinière AGA ancienne. La cheminée date du début du 20ᵉ siècle.*
PAGE DE DROITE: *Déplacer une cuisinière AGA en fonte émaillée style fifties n'est pas un jeu d'enfants. Les propriétaires de ce cottage irlandais ont préféré la laisser où elle était.*
DOUBLE PAGE SUI-VANTE: *Dans un château en Hollande, cet ancien four maçonné a été revêtu de carreaux de Delft blancs.*

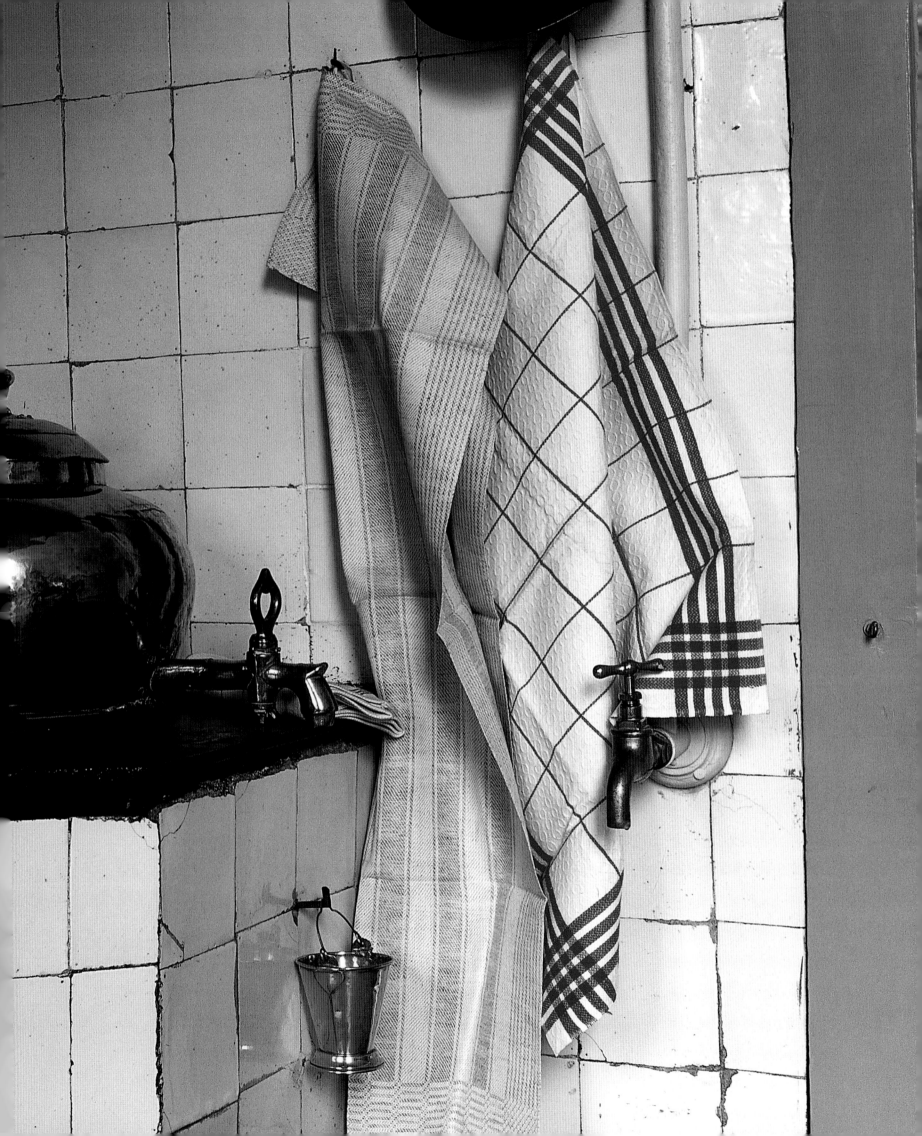

LEFT: *In this old farm-house kitchen, the table is the main work sur-face. The brick floor is both attractive and easy to maintain.*
FACING PAGE: *The owner of this Mallorcan fisherman's cottage has made a kitchen space by equipping an "oriental" niche with a basic gas cooker.*

LINKS: *Hauptarbeits-fläche in dieser alten Bauernküche ist der Tisch. Der Backstein-boden ist so hübsch wie pflegeleicht.*
RECHTE SEITE: *In seinem kleinen Fischer-haus auf Mallorca hat der Besitzer in einer »orientalischen« Nische eine Kochecke einge-richtet und dort einen einfachen Gaskocher aufgestellt.*

A GAUCHE: *Dans la cuisine d'une ferme ancienne, la table est devenue une véritable table de travail. Le sol en briques est joli et facile à entretenir.*
PAGE DE DROITE: *Dans sa petite maison de pêcheur à Majorque, le propriétaire a créé un coin cuisine en équi-pant une niche «orien-tale» de la plus simple des cuisinières à gaz.*

ABOVE: *The ink-blue of the panels is echoed by the sober 1900 sideboard.*

RIGHT: *a delicious soup simmering on the wood stove.*

FACING PAGE: *At Loughcrew, the owners have surrounded their Aga cooker with black and beige tiles.*

FOLLOWING PAGES: *At the Evennous' house, the yellow walls set off the humble kitchen utensils. The brick shelves were made by Franck; Marianne sewed the curtains.*

OBEN: *Das Tintenblau der Wandverkleidung kehrt in der schlichten Anrichte wieder.*

RECHTS: *Eine köstliche Suppe köchelt auf dem Holzofen.*

RECHTE SEITE: *In Loughcrew haben die Eigentümer ihren AGA-Herd mit beigeschwarzen Kacheln umrahmt.*

FOLGENDE DOPPELSEITE: *Im Haus der Evennous bringen die gelben Wände die Küchengeräte zur Geltung. Franck hat die Backsteinregale gebaut und Marianne die Vorhänge genäht.*

CI-DESSUS: *Le bleu encre des lambris se répète dans le sobre buffet 1900.*

A DROITE: *Une délicieuse soupe mijote sur la cuisinière à bois.*

PAGE DE DROITE: *A Loughcrew, les propriétaires ont entouré leur AGA de carreaux beiges et noirs.*

DOUBLE PAGE SUIVANTE: *Chez les Evennou, les murs jaunes mettent en valeur des ustensiles modestes. Franck a construit les rangements de brique et Marianne a cousu les rideaux.*

PAGES 120–121: *In this Mallorcan kitchen, the old stone sink has been lovingly preserved. The yellow walls reflect the sunlight.*

PREVIOUS PAGES: *The traditional curtain contrasts with the yellow walls surrounding this 18th century stone sink.*

ABOVE: *This bulky 19th century cupboard is home to an assortment of period earthenware and plates. The pine wood kitchen table is easily maintained, by scrubbing with sand and soapy water.*

SEITEN 120–121: *In dieser mallorquinischen Küche wurde die alte Steinspüle erhalten. Die gelben Wände reflektieren das Sonnenlicht.*

VORHERGEHENDE DOPPELSEITE: *Der traditionelle Vorhang kontrastiert mit den gelben Wänden rund um die Steinspüle aus dem 18. Jahrhundert.*

OBEN: *Der Schrank aus dem 19. Jahrhundert birgt historische Fayencen und Geschirrwaren. Der pflegeleichte Kiefernholztisch wird mit Sand und Seifenwasser gescheuert.*

PAGES 120–121: *Dans cette cuisine majorquine, les habitants ont voulu garder l'ancien évier en pierre. Des murs, peints en jaune, font entrer le soleil.*

DOUBLE PAGE PRECEDENTE: *Le rideau traditionnel contraste avec les murs jaunes qui entourent un évier en pierre 18ᵉ.*

CI-DESSUS: *L'armoire 19ᵉ abrite une collection de faïences et de vaisselle d'époque. La table de cuisine en pin est facile à entretenir et on la récure à la brosse en chiendent avec du sable et de l'eau savonneuse.*

FACING PAGE: *These days, the copper washbasin and its pretty beaten copper tank have lost none of their beauty or usefulness.*

RECHTE SEITE: *Das kupferne Handwaschbecken und der gehämmerte Wassertank aus demselben Material haben nichts von ihrer Schönheit und Zweckmäßigkeit eingebüßt.*

PAGE DE DROITE: *De nos jours, le lavemains en cuivre et sa jolie citerne martelée n'ont rien perdu de leur beauté et de leur aspect fonctionnel.*

This 17th century painting illustrates some of the classic elements of a good table: a silk tablecloth and a linen runner with embroidered edges.

Dieses Gemälde aus dem 17. Jahrhundert zeigt klassisches Zubehör einer schönen Tafel: ein Seidentischtuch und einen Leinenläufer mit Spitzenbordüren.

Ce tableau d'époque 17ᵉ présente les éléments classiques et luxueux qui font la belle table: nappe en soie damassée et «couloir» en lin damassé bordé de dentelle.

The antique dealer Rob Bruil and his wife Marieke have preserved the authentic aspect of this charming Dutch kitchen, side by side with a slate sink and a resolutely contemporary hotplate set into a painted wood surface.

Der Antiquitätenhändler Rob Bruil und seine Frau Marieke haben das Authentische dieser charmanten holländischen Küche gewahrt und es durch eine in die lackierte Holzarbeitsfläche eingelassene Schieferspüle sowie ein ausgesprochen modernes Kochmodul ergänzt.

L'antiquaire Rob Bruil et sa femme Marieke ont préservé l'aspect authentique de cette charmante cuisine hollandaise tout en encastrant un évier en ardoise et une plaque chauffante résolument contemporaine dans le plan de travail en pin et en bois peint.

LEFT: *Wooden sinks
are rare nowadays. But
because they are gentle
on delicate china and
glass, they still have
their place in the kit-
chens of great houses:
here, for example, at
Twickel Castle in the
Netherlands.*
FACING PAGE: *a slate
sink beside the window
in a huge 17th century
Tuscan kitchen. The
flower-patterned cur-
tain conceals shelves
loaded with crockery.*

LINKS: *Holzspülen
sind heutzutage eine
Seltenheit. Weil sie aber
empfindliches Porzel-
langeschirr und Gläser
schonen, haben sie in
Küchen großer Häuser
noch immer ihren Platz,
hier zum Beispiel auf
Schloss Twickel in den
Niederlanden.*
RECHTE SEITE: *eine
Schieferspüle am Fens-
ter einer geräumigen
toskanischen Küche aus
dem 17. Jahrhundert.
Hinter dem geblümten
Vorhang verbergen sich
Regale voller Geschirr.*

A GAUCHE: *Les éviers
en bois sont rares au-
jourd'hui. Doux aux
porcelaines et aux verres
délicats, ils ont souvent
leur place dans les cui-
sines des grandes mai-
sons – ici, par exemple
au château de Twickel
aux Pays-Bas.*
PAGE DE DROITE:
*L'évier en schiste se
trouve près de la fenêtre
dans une vaste cuisine
toscane d'époque 17ᵉ,
car la cuisinière a tou-
jours besoin de lumière
pour travailler. Le ri-
deau à fleurs cache des
étagères à vaisselle.*

LEFT: *A trio of coloured tiles brightens the monochrome surface above this stone sink.*
FACING PAGE: *a rough plank used as a shelf for earthenware, bottles and wicker baskets.*
FOLLOWING PAGES: *In this Mallorcan kitchen, the sink occupies its own niche. Cups, bowls and other earthenware stand on the plastered shelves.*

LINKS: *Ein Trio farbiger Fliesen hellt die unifarbene Kachelung über diesem Spülstein auf.*
RECHTE SEITE: *Ein schlichtes Brett bildet die Ablage für Steingut, Flaschen und Weidenkörbe.*
FOLGENDE DOPPELSEITE: *In diesem mallorquinischen Haus hat der Spülstein seine eigene Nische erhalten. Auf den Ablagen aus Gips stehen Tassen, Schüsseln und andere Steingutgefäße.*

A GAUCHE: *Un trio de carreaux colorés anime un carrelage uni au-dessus de cet évier en pierre.*
PAGE DE DROITE: *Une simple planche brute sert à ranger des faïences, des bouteilles et des paniers en osier.*
DOUBLE PAGE SUIVANTE: *Dans cette cuisine à Majorque, une niche en stuc abrite un évier en pierre. Sur les rangements enduits de stuc sont disposés des coupes, des bols et d'autres récipients en faïence.*

PREVIOUS PAGES: *This stone sink is deliberately shallow: perfect for rinsing and cleaning fish, shellfish and crustaceans.*
LEFT: *The Dutch are masters of the art of still life, as this fine composition shows.*
FACING PAGE: *In this Suffolk barn, the owner has set a stone sink into a masonry work surface.*

VORHERGEHENDE DOPPELSEITE: *Dieser Spülstein eignet sich perfekt zum Wässern und Putzen von Fisch und Schalentieren.*
LINKS: *Die Niederländer sind Meister des Still-Lebens, wie diese fein gearbeitete Komposition zeigt.*
RECHTE SEITE: *In dieser Scheune in Suffolk hat der Hausherr den Spülstein in das Sichtmauerwerk eingelassen.*

DOUBLE PAGE PRECEDENTE: *Cet évier en pierre est peu profond et parfait pour rincer et nettoyer des poissons, des coquillages et des crustacés.*
A GAUCHE: *Les Hollandais sont les maîtres incontestés de la nature morte et cette belle composition en est la preuve.*
PAGE DE DROITE: *Dans une grange au cœur du Suffolk, le propriétaire a encastré un évier en pierre dans un plan de travail maçonné.*

CROCKERY
& UTENSILS

We are always moved by spacious old kitchens, wherein the eye is irresistibly drawn to a noble battery of coppers lined on a shelf or hung within reach around the stove hood. We love the purity of their forms and the beauty of their materials.

Likewise a kitchen whose bare-beamed ceiling is almost hidden by straw baskets is deeply reassuring to the person working in it; and when you see a dresser stuffed with plates, soup bowls, butter dishes and cake moulds made of enameled earthenware and terracotta, or note with surprise that a kitchen built at the dawn of the third millennium still has a kettle sputtering on a wood-fired hob, ready for making the coffee from beans ground three times over in an old hand mill – well, then you understand that romance is still alive.

Behind the oak door with its peephole is an old pantry, cool as the vaulted cellar of a notary. Between these four white washed walls are pots of homemade jam with handwritten labels that make the mouth water, along with baskets filled with vegetables, eggs and fruit.

GESCHIRR & KÜCHENUTENSILIEN

VAISSELLE & USTENSILES DE CUISINE

Stets empfinden wir etwas Besonderes in geräumigen alten Küchen, in denen der Blick unwiderstehlich von einer stattlichen Batterie Kupfergeschirr angezogen wird, die auf einem Bord aufgereiht oder in Reichweite um die Abzugshaube aufgehängt ist. Die Reinheit der Formen und die Schönheit des Materials ziehen uns an.

Und eine Küche, deren Balkendecke unter den daran befestigten Weidekörben schier verschwindet, hat gewiss etwas ungemein Beruhigendes für denjenigen, der in ihr arbeitet. Wenn man dann noch eine Anrichte voller Teller, Suppenschüsseln, Butterdosen und Kuchenformen aus emailliertem Steingut und Terrakotta sieht und erstaunt feststellt, dass eine Ende des zweiten Jahrtausends gebaute Küche nach wie vor mit einem Kessel aufwartet, der auf einem Holzofen pfeift und darauf wartet, die in einer alten Mühle dreifach gemahlenen Kaffeebohnen aufzubrühen, dann begreift man, dass Romantik nicht von gestern ist.

Hinter der Eichentür mit dem vergitterten Bullauge tut sich eine alte Vorratskammer mit gekälkten Wänden auf, kühl wie das Kellergewölbe eines herrschaftlichen Hauses. Hier stehen Körbe voller Gemüse, Eier und Obst und handbeschriftete Töpfe mit selbst gemachter Marmelade, bei deren Anblick einem das Wasser im Munde zusammenläuft.

On les aime bien, ces grandes cuisines anciennes où l'œil est irrésistiblement attiré par l'imposante batterie en cuivre posée sur une étagère ou accrochée, à portée de la main, à la hotte de la cheminée. Et on se laisse vite séduire par la pureté de leurs formes et par la beauté de leurs matières.

Une cuisine dont le plafond à poutres apparentes est presque dissimulé par une avalanche de paniers en osier, rassure celui qui y travaille. Après avoir caressé du regard un dressoir regorgeant d'assiettes, de soupières, de beurriers et de moules à gâteaux en faïence et en terre cuite émaillée et constaté avec surprise qu'une cuisine née à l'aube du troisième millénaire n'a pas renié la bouilloire qui chantonne sur un poêle à bois et le café moulu – trois fois – dans un vieux moulin à café, on comprend que le romantisme ne fait pas partie d'une époque révolue.

Derrière la porte en chêne équipée d'un hublot garni d'une moustiquaire dort le garde-manger d'antan, frais comme la cave voûtée d'une maison de notaire. Entre ses quatre murs blanchis à la chaux, on ne s'étonne plus de trouver des pots de confiture maison, dont les étiquettes écrites à la main mettent l'eau à la bouche et des paniers remplis de légumes, d'œufs et de fruits. Qu'attendons-nous pour goûter à ces trésors?

CROCKERY
& UTENSILS

GESCHIRR
& KÜCHEN-
UTENSILIEN

VAISSELLE &
USTENSILES
DE CUISINE

PREVIOUS PAGES:
An old-style kitchen can do without coppers – provided it has good tin utensils to take their place.
ABOVE: *Ladles made of copper, tin or aluminium are a must in every kitchen.*
RIGHT: *Fine old crockery is the pride of every housewife.*
FACING PAGE: *In this drawer, the knives and forks are laid out separately in old tin boxes. Wicker or rattan baskets serve the purpose equally well.*

VORHERGEHENDE DOPPELSEITE:
Eine Küche alten Stils kommt auch ohne Kupfer aus, wenn es stattdessen gute Geräte aus Weißblech gibt.
OBEN: *Schaumkellen aus Kupfer, Weißblech oder Aluminium sind aus der Küche nicht mehr wegzudenken.*
RECHTS: *Schönes altes Geschirr ist der Stolz jeder Hausfrau.*
RECHTE SEITE: *In dieser Schublade sind Messer und Gabeln in alten Zinnkästchen abgelegt. Weiden- oder Rattankörbe erfüllen diesen Zweck ebenfalls.*

DOUBLE PAGE PRE-CEDENTE: *Une cuisine à l'ancienne peut se passer de batterie en cuivre si elle peut s'enorgueillir d'ustensiles en fer blanc.*
CI-DESSUS: *En cuivre, en fer blanc ou en aluminium, peu importe, car les écumoires font dorénavant partie de notre vie quotidienne.*
A DROITE: *La belle vaisselle ancienne fait la fierté des ménagères.*
PAGE DE DROITE: *Dans ce tiroir, les couverts sont rangés dans de vieilles gamelles en fer blanc. On peut aussi ranger couteaux et fourchettes dans des paniers en rotin ou en osier.*

Zimmt.

Gemürz.

Gries

PREVIOUS PAGES: *The old inscribed vessels are both decorative and practical.*
LEFT: *a built-in cupboard, with 19th century Paris dishes. A period cupboard can also be turned into a display cabinet by putting in old-style open metalwork.*
FACING PAGE: *In this spacious Touraine kitchen, the owner has set out a fine 18th century service on long shelves above the work surface.*

VORHERGEHENDE DOPPELSEITEN: *Die alten Gefäße mit Aufschrift sind sehr dekorativ und praktisch.*
LINKS: *ein Einbauschrank mit Pariser Porzellangeschirr aus dem 19. Jahrhundert. Mit Hilfe von Metallgittern nach alter Art lässt sich das gute Stück auch zur Vitrine umfunktionieren.*
RECHTE SEITE: *In dieser großen Küche in der Touraine bewahrt der Hausherr sein Service aus dem 18. Jahrhundert in einem langen Hängeschrank über der Arbeitsfläche auf.*

DOUBLE PAGES PRECEDENTES: *Les inscriptions de ces anciens récipients en font des objets pratiques et très décoratifs.*
A GAUCHE: *Une armoire encastrée abrite une vaisselle en porcelaine de Paris 19ᵉ. On peut aussi transformer une armoire d'époque en vitrine en y incorporant des grillages à l'ancienne.*
PAGE DE DROITE: *Dans cette grande cuisine tourangelle, le propriétaire a disposé son beau service 18ᵉ sur de longues étagères accrochées au-dessus du plan de travail.*

ABOVE: *The Dutch decorator Hans Hesseling has built display cupboards on either side of this double door.*
RIGHT: *The grey and white of a Louis Seize corner cabinet goes well with the cream and ox-blood tones.*
FACING PAGE: *a 19th century cupboard containing a service of fine porcelain.*
FOLLOWING PAGES: *An old cupboard can be used for storing dishes, plates, bowls or whatever you like, provided there's some kind of harmony in the colours.*

OBEN: *Die Tür wird von Vitrinen flankiert, die der niederländische Dekorateur Hans Hesseling gebaut hat.*
RECHTS: *Das Grau und Weiß des Louis-Seize-Schranks harmoniert mit den Creme- und Ochsenbluttönen.*
RECHTE SEITE: *ein Schrank aus dem 19. Jahrhundert mit feinem Porzellan.*
FOLGENDE DOPPEL-SEITE: *In einem alten Schrank können Schüsseln, Teller oder auch anderes aufbewahrt werden, wenn die Farben harmonieren.*

CI-DESSUS: *Le décorateur hollandais Hans Hesseling a construit des armoires-vitrines de chaque côté d'une double porte.*
A DROITE: *Le gris et le blanc de l'encoignure Louis Seize s'harmonisent avec les tons crème et sang de bœuf.*
PAGE DE DROITE: *Une armoire 19e héberge un beau service en porcelaine.*
DOUBLE PAGE SUIVANTE: *Une armoire ancienne peut abriter un beau service à vaisselle ou être remplie d'autres objets, pourvu qu'il y ait une subtile harmonie de couleurs.*

PREVIOUS PAGES: *The dishes show well against the grey-green of this corner cupboard.* LEFT: *an old school coat rack, now used for a different purpose.* FACING PAGE: *Old chocolate boxes were the inspiration for this décor.* FOLLOWING PAGES: *a Victorian service in an Athens kitchen, and the floor of a kitchen decorated with imitation worn tiles.*

VORHERGEHENDE DOPPELSEITE: *Vor dem grüngrauen Schrank kommt das Geschirr gut zur Geltung.* LINKS: *eine alte Schulgarderobe mit neuer Funktion.* RECHTE SEITE: *Alte Schokoladenkisten haben zu diesem Dekor angeregt.* FOLGENDE DOPPELSEITE: *ein viktorianisches Service in einer Athener Küche und ein Küchenfußboden, der einem Steinplattenbelag nachempfunden ist.*

DOUBLE PAGE PRECEDENTE: *La vaisselle rend bien sur le vert-de-gris de cette encoignure.* A GAUCHE: *Un ancien portemanteau d'école a trouvé une nouvelle fonction.* PAGE DE DROITE: *D'anciennes boîtes de chocolat ont inspiré ce décor.* DOUBLE PAGE SUIVANTE: *un service à café au décor victorien dans une cuisine d'Athènes et le plancher d'une cuisine decoré de fausses dalles usées.*

PAGES 160 AND
161: *a Dutch farm-
house with an early
20th century cast iron
stove and an amusing
assortment of dishes.*
PAGE 162: *old
earthenware, beauti-
fully arranged on min-
imalist shelving.*
PAGE 163: *kitchen
utensils on fleur de lys
hooks against a pale
wood background.*
RIGHT: *The dark green
walls and shelves offset
a collection of utensils,
plates and copper cake
moulds.*

SEITE 160 UND
161: *ein niederländi-
sches Bauernhaus mit
einem gusseisernen
Ofen vom Anfang des
20. Jahrhunderts und
lustigem Geschirr.*
SEITE 162: *alte Fay-
encen, geschmackvoll
auf minimalistischen
Borden arrangiert.*
SEITE 163: *Töpfe an
lilienblütenförmigen
Haken vor hellem
Holzhintergrund.*
RECHTS: *Die dunkel-
grünen Wände lassen
die kupfernen Geräte,
Teller und Kuchenfor-
men schön zur Geltung
kommen.*

PAGES 160 ET 161:
*une ferme hollandaise
avec un poêle en fonte
du début du 20e siècle et
une vaisselle amusante.*
PAGE 162: *des faïen-
ces anciennes disposées
avec goût sur des étagè-
res minimalistes.*
PAGE 163: *une batte-
rie de cuisine aux parois
blondes avec des crochets
«fleurdelisés».*
A DROITE: *Les murs et
les étagères vert foncé
font ressortir la batterie
de cuisine, les plats et les
moules à cake en cuivre.*

ABOVE: *The sand-col-oured walls and grey-green furniture and shelving are an inspir-ation to anyone with dreams of a period kit-chen of their own.*
RIGHT: *In this Suffolk manor house, the cop-pers hang from game racks attached to the ceiling.*
FACING PAGE: *The decorator Jacques Gar-cia has recreated the original kitchen with things found in antique shops. The grey-blue paneling and the "Bur-gundy stone" colour of the plasterwork are typical of the region.*

OBEN: *Die sandfarbe-nen Wände sowie die graugrünen Möbel und Borde sind eine Inspira-tionsquelle für alle, die von einer eigenen histo-rischen Küche träumen.*
RECHTS: *In diesem Suffolker Herrenhaus hängt das Kupfergerät von einem Jagdgestänge herab.*
RECHTE SEITE: *De-korateur Jacques Garcia hat die Originalküche mit Fundstücken aus Antiquariaten wieder hergerichtet. Die grau-blaue Täfelung und der burgundersteinfarbene Verputz sind typisch für die Region.*

CI-DESSUS: *Les murs couleur sable et ses meubles et ses étagères gris vert peuvent inspi-rer ceux qui rêvent de se construire une cuisine d'époque.*
A DROITE: *Dans son manoir du Suffolk, le propriétaire accroche les cuivres à des tringles à gibier.*
PAGE DE DROITE: *Le décorateur Jacques Garcia a recréé la cui-sine d'époque en chi-nant chez les antiquai-res. Le ton gris bleu des boiseries et le stuc cou-leur «pierre de Bour-gogne» sont typiques de la région.*

LEFT: *against the oak panelling, a hunting trophy and a copper saucepan lid.*
FACING PAGE: *Anna and Gunther Lambert's guest house has a pretty sideboard filled with blue and white earthenware and utensils of various kinds.*

LINKS: *An der mit Eichenholz vertäfelten Wand hängen eine Jagdtrophäe und ein Kupferdeckel.*
RECHTE SEITE: *In ihrem Gästehaus haben Anna und Gunther Lambert eine schöne alte Anrichte mit blauweißem Steingutgeschirr sowie mit Utensilien aus Kupfer und Korb gefüllt.*

A GAUCHE: *Sur les lambris en chêne, un trophée de chasse et un couvercle en cuivre font l'éloge des plaisirs domestiques dans un château 18ᵉ.*
PAGE DE DROITE: *Dans leur maison d'amis, Anna et Gunther Lambert ont rempli un joli buffet ancien de faïences bleues et blanches et d'ustensiles en cuivre et en osier.*

FACING PAGE: *This contemporary kitchen in Paris owes its charm to its colour scheme: white tiles on the walls, beige and ox-blood on the floor, pale furniture and wickerwork.*
ABOVE: *In this larder of a Swedish castle, broad, roomy shelves are stacked with baskets, glasses and jars.*
RIGHT: *an old country coat rack filled with terracotta jugs, baskets and shopping bags.*
FOLLOWING PAGES: *in the annex of an 18th century kitchen, an old sink surrounded by shelves.*

LINKE SEITE: *Diese Pariser Küche verdankt ihren Charme den Farben: weiße Kacheln an den Wänden, Beige und Ochsenblut auf dem Boden, helle Möbel und Korbwaren.*
OBEN: *In dieser Speisekammer eines schwedischen Schlosses stehen die Regale voller Körbe.*
RECHTS: *eine alte Garderobe mit Terrakottakrügen, Körben und Einkaufstaschen.*
FOLGENDE DOPPELSEITE: *Die alte Spüle im Anbau einer Küche aus dem 18. Jahrhundert umgeben Regale.*

PAGE DE GAUCHE: *Cette cuisine à Paris doit son charme à ses teintes délicates: carreaux blancs sur les murs, beige et sang-de-bœuf sur le sol, mobilier blond et vanneries.*
CI-DESSUS: *Dans ce garde-manger d'un château suédois, des étagères hautes et larges abritent des paniers.*
A DROITE: *un ancien portemanteau rustique avec des jarres en terre cuite et des paniers.*
DOUBLE PAGE SUIVANTE: *Dans l'annexe d'une cuisine 18e, un vieil évier est entouré d'étagères.*

DECORATION & FLOWERS

An old kitchen is never ostentatious in its décor. Its furnishings are modest and it favours oil lamps and hanging tin chandeliers over electric light. Whether you find it in Burgundy, on an obscure Greek island, in remotest Somerset, on a hilltop overlooking Florence, in an Austrian chalet that looks like a cuckoo clock, in a Mallorcan "finca" or a Dutch manor house, such a kitchen remains a steadfast bastion of tradition.

The walls may be white, blue or plain stone, but they are invariably coupled with stout furniture, a check tablecloth, homely curtains and inside shutters. All in all, the kitchen seems to know that it's a good place to be. Its willingness to please is expressed by huge sideboards groaning with dishes, or by the monotonous tick, tock of a moon-faced clock; there may also be brightly-coloured prints of Christian saints, idealized views of distant lands, and perhaps the silhouette of a prize bull from the year 1889.

On the table, a stoneware vase drips flowers picked in the garden, by the vegetable patch. There are daisies, daffodils in season, and roses on Sundays, poppies and cornflowers too, brought in because their colours go well with the painted furniture, or simply because people in the country make bouquets with whatever nature provides.

DEKORATION & BLUMEN

Eine alte Küche wird nie prunkvoll dekoriert sein. Ihre Möblierung ist bescheiden, und statt elektrischem Licht werden Petroleumlampen und Kerzen in Blechkandelabern bevorzugt. Gleich ob im Burgund, auf einer abgelegenen griechischen Insel, im hintersten Somerset, in einem österreichischen Bauernhaus, das einer Kuckucksuhr gleicht, auf einer mallorquinischen Finca oder in einem holländischen Herrenhaus – eine solche Küche bleibt eine verlässliche Hochburg der Tradition.

Ihre Wände mögen weiß sein, blau oder aus Sichtstein, durchweg wird sie mit robusten Möbeln, dem vertrauten Karotischtuch, wohnlichen Vorhängen und Fensterläden aufwarten. Sie scheint geradezu zu wissen, dass sie gemütlich ist und ihr Wunsch gefallen zu wollen äußert sich in großen, vor Geschirr fast berstenden Anrichten und im monotonen Ticktack einer kreisrunden Pendeluhr. Vielleicht gibt es auch buntfarbige Drucke christlicher Heiliger, idealisierte Ansichten ferner Länder oder einfach eine Darstellung des Preisochsen von 1889.

In der Steingutvase auf dem Tisch stehen immer frisch gepflückte Blumen, die neben dem Gemüsebeet im eigenen Garten wachsen: je nach Jahreszeit Margariten oder Narzissen und sonntags Rosen, aber manchmal auch Mohn und Kornblumen, weil deren Farben so schön zu den bemalten Möbeln passen, oder einfach, weil auf dem Land Blumensträuße aus dem bestehen, was die Natur hergibt.

DECORATION & FLEURS

Son décor n'est jamais ostentatoire, ses meubles sont modestes et elle préfère la lampe à pétrole et la suspension en tôle équipée de bougies à l'ampoule électrique … Qu'elle se trouve en Bourgogne, sur une île grecque obscure, dans le fin fond du Somerset, sur une colline qui surplombe Florence, en Autriche dans un chalet aux allures de «coucou» ou qu'elle se cache derrière les murs épais d'une finca majorquine ou d'un manoir hollandais, la cuisine ancienne reste fidèle à ses traditions.

Que les murs soient crépis de blanc, bleu vif ou en pierre apparente, ils se marient invariablement avec des meubles robustes, la nappe à carreaux familière, les rideaux de bonne femme ou les volets intérieurs. La cuisine sait qu'il fait bon vivre près d'elle, et son désir de plaire s'exprime par ces grands buffets bourrés de vaisselle, par le tic-tac monotone de l'horloge ronde comme un œil de pigeon et par ces gravures qui représentent des saints aux couleurs de bonbon, des vues idéalisées de pays lointains ou simplement le Bœuf Couronné de l'année 1889.

Sur la table, un vase en grès accueille des fleurs cueillies dans le jardin, près du potager. Des marguerites, des jonquilles, quand c'est la saison, ou des roses, le dimanche. Parfois des pavots ou des bleuets, parce que leur couleur se marie bien avec celle du mobilier peint ou pour la simple raison, qu'à la campagne, on compose les bouquets avec ce que la nature a envie d'offrir …

DECORATION & FLOWERS

DEKORATION & BLUMEN

DECORATION & FLEURS

PREVIOUS PAGES:
*Willem van Aelst,
Flower Vase and Fob
Watch, 1663, oil on
canvas, Mauritshuis,
The Hague.*
FACING PAGE: *in an
authentic 1900 kitchen,
a bunch of amaryllis
with royal blue and
white furniture.*
ABOVE: *parrot tulips
and oriental-inspired
blue and white crockery
in the Edinburgh house
shared by Jimmy Tom-
son and David Gillon.*
RIGHT: *An earthenware
jug awaits the ideal
bouquet.*

VORHERGEHENDE
DOPPELSEITE:
*Willem van Aelst,
Blumenvase und
Taschenuhr, 1663, Öl
auf Leinwand, Mau-
ritshuis, Den Haag.*
LINKE SEITE: *In die-
ser Küche aus dem 19.
Jahrhundert wurde ein
Strauß Amaryllis mit
weißen und königsblau-
en Möbeln kombiniert.*
OBEN: *Papageien-
tulpen und orientalisch
inspiriertes blauweißes
Porzellan in der Küche
von Jimmy Tomson und
David Gillon in Edin-
burgh.*
RECHTS: *Ein Stein-
gutkrug wartet auf den
idealen Blumenstrauß.*

DOUBLE PAGE PRE-
CEDENTE: *Willem van
Aelst, Vase à fleurs et
montre de poche, 1663,
huile sur toile, Maurits-
huis, La Haye.*
PAGE DE GAUCHE:
*Dans cette cuisine d'é-
poque 1900, un bouquet
d'amaryllis côtoie des
meubles blancs et bleu
roi.*
CI-DESSUS: *Dans la
cuisine de Jimmy Tom-
son et David Gillon à
Edimbourg, les tulipes
perroquets saluent
une vaisselle bleue et
blanche d'inspiration
orientale.*
A DROITE: *Une cruche
en faïence attend le
bouquet idéal.*

PAGES 180 AND 181: variegated tulips and poppies in a simple earthenware jug and a Baroque lead vase.

PAGE 182: In this refined kitchen the sober floral composition echoes the golden-brown madeleines.

PAGE 183: Dennis Severs' modest fireplace is decorated with newspaper: a fine example of "arte povera".

PREVIOUS PAGES: A bouquet of radishes against a striped yellow background. The orange spiked with cloves is there to scent the air.

FACING PAGE: In this stylist's kitchen, the bouquet of sunflowers enlivens the beige and yellow décor, setting the tone for an ambiance that is both eclectic and eccentric.

ABOVE: yellow tulips in a champagne bucket, in the kitchen of an Amsterdam couturier.

FOLLOWING PAGES: In this kitchen, the brightly-coloured tablecloth and the earthenware bowl filled with earthenware fruit supply a note of gaiety and freshness.

SEITE 180 UND 181: gesprenkelte Tulpen in einem schlichten Krug und Mohnblumen in einer barocken Bleivase.

SEITE 182: Die Blumenkomposition ergänzt die goldbraunen Madeleines.

SEITE 183: Dennis Severs' bescheidener Kamin ist mit einer Zeitung dekoriert: ein treffendes Beispiel für »arte povera«.

VORHERGEHENDE DOPPELSEITE: ein Radieschenstrauß vor gelb gestreiftem Hintergrund. Die mit Nelken gespickte Orange verströmt ihren Duft.

LINKE SEITE: In der Küche eines Designers belebt ein Strauß Sonnenblumen das beige und gelbe Dekor und bestimmt das eklektisch-exzentrische Ambiente.

OBEN: gelbe Tulpen in einem Champagnerkübel in der Küche eines Amsterdamer Modeschöpfers.

FOLGENDE DOPPELSEITE: In dieser Küche setzen die bunte Tischdecke und die Steingutschale mit Früchtenachbildungen aus demselben Material eine Note heiterer Frische.

PAGES 180 ET 181: Les tulipes panachées et les coquelicots s'accommodent d'une cruche et d'un vase en plomb aux allures baroques.

PAGE 182: Dans cette cuisine raffinée, la sobre composition florale fait écho aux madeleines dorées.

PAGE 183: Chez Dennis Severs, la cheminée modeste est ornée d'un volant découpé dans un journal: un bel exemple d'«Arte povera».

DOUBLE PAGE PRECEDENTE: Un bouquet de radis sur fond jaune rayé. L'orange piquée de clous de girofle parfume l'air.

PAGE DE GAUCHE: Dans la cuisine d'un styliste, le bouquet de tournesols anime le décor beige et blond et réussit à dominer une décoration à la fois éclectique et excentrique.

CI-DESSUS: Des tulipes jaunes explosent dans un seau à champagne dans la cuisine d'un couturier à Amsterdam.

DOUBLE PAGE SUIVANTE: Dans cette cuisine où règne le clair-obscur, la nappe très colorée et la coupe en faïence remplie d'un trompe-l'œil de fruits dans la même matière, apportent une note de fraîcheur et de gaieté.

PREVIOUS PAGES: *a speckled enamel coffee pot against a Delft tableau and an embroidered glass-cloth.*
RIGHT: *The check tablecloth is all very well; but a few olive sprays in a jug is something out of the ordinary.*
FOLLOWING PAGES: *fruit on a tea-tray and transformed into exquisite jams. Nearby, a branch from an apple tree sticking out of a pitcher.*

VORHERGEHENDE DOPPELSEITE: *eine Kaffeekanne aus Email vor einem Tableau aus Delfter Porzellan und ein besticktes Geschirrtuch.*
RECHTS: *Der Krug mit den Olivenzweigen verleiht dem Arrangement mit dem karierten Tischtuch etwas Außergewöhnliches.*
FOLGENDE DOPPELSEITE: *Früchte auf einem Teetablett, erlesene Konfitüren und ein Apfelbaumzweig in einer Kanne.*

DOUBLE PAGE PRECEDENTE: *une cafetière en émail moucheté devant un tableau en Delft et un essuie-verres brodé.*
A DROITE: *D'accord pour la nappe à carreaux. Mais quelques branches d'olivier dans un pichet, voilà qui sort de l'ordinaire.*
DOUBLE PAGE SUIVANTE: *Les fruits s'attardent sur un plateau à thé et se transforment en confitures exquises. Une branche de pommier dans son broc nous fait même un clin d'œil.*

ACKNOWLEDGEMENTS

DANKSAGUNG

REMERCIEMENTS

To render sufficient thanks to all those whose care and hard work have been invested into the kitchens shown here would be quite simply impossible. For us, the making of this book has been a romantic voyage into the past by way of the images in our archives; and now that the job is done, we can say that we have truly begun to understand the vital place in all our daily lives that is occupied by the kitchen. So our heartfelt thanks go out to Cordula, Emma and Heiltje, our grandmothers and great grandmothers, in whose venerable kitchens we first learned to love and revere good, traditional cooking.

All denen namentlich zu danken, deren Küchen wir in diesem Buch für die Nachwelt festhalten durften, ist kaum möglich. Als wir unsere Archive durchforsteten und so viele romantische Bilder vor unseren Augen vorbeizogen, erlebten wir eine wundervolle Reise in die Vergangenheit. Erst heute, nachdem wir dieses Buch erstellt haben, ist uns klar geworden, welche Rolle die Küche in unserem alltäglichen Leben spielt. Unser besonderer Dank gilt Cordula, unserer Urgroßmutter, sowie Emma und Heiltje, unseren Großmüttern, in deren unvergesslichen Küchen wir die gute Kochkunst von einst kennen und schätzen gelernt haben.

Remercier tous ceux qui nous ont permis d'immortaliser leur cuisine est impossible. Puisant dans nos archives et voyant défiler devant nos yeux autant d'images impregnées de romantisme et de nostalgie fut pour nous un délicieux voyage dans le passé. Et ce n'est qu'aujourd'hui à travers la réalisation de ce livre que nous comprenons quelle place importante occupe la cuisine dans notre vie quotidienne. Merci à Cordula, à Emma et à Heiltje, nos arrière-grand-mères et grands-mères – qui nous ont appris à aimer la bonne cuisine d'antan au sein de leurs vieilles cuisines inoubliables.

Barbara & René Stoeltie

TASCHEN'S COUNTRY HOUSES

Edited by Angelika Taschen

Barbara & René Stoeltie

PUBLISHED:

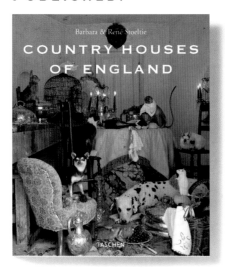

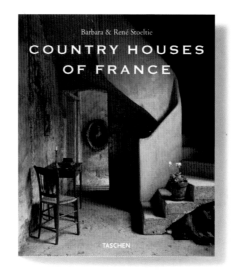

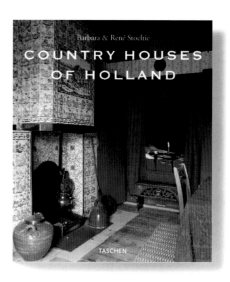

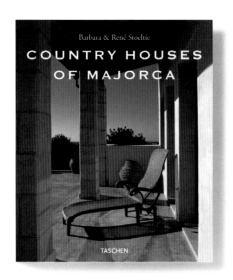

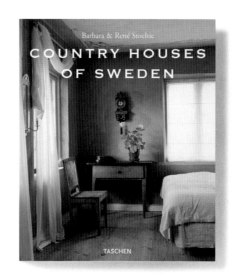

"'Decorator porn,' a friend calls it, those sensuous photograph books of beautiful houses. Long on details and atmosphere and packed with ideas, this is a bountiful look at beautiful but unpretentious homes in the place where 'everything is founded on the link between beauty and well-being.' It's easy to linger there."

The Virginian-Pilot, USA

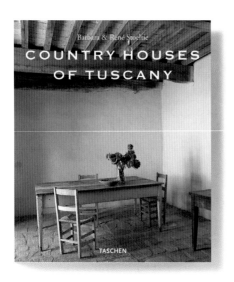

IN PREPARATION:

Country Bathrooms

Country Bedrooms

Country Houses of Ireland

Country Houses of Morocco

Country Houses of New England

Country Houses of Portugal

Country Houses of Provence

Country Houses of Russia